Guide to Audit
Data Analytics

D1570252

23723-349

Preface

Notice to Readers

AICPA *Guide to Audit Data Analytics* has been developed by the AICPA Audit Data Analytics Working Group to provide an introduction and overview of data analytic techniques to assist financial statement auditors in applying such techniques in performing their audit engagements.

This publication is an *other auditing publication* as defined in AU-C section 200, *Overall Objectives of the Independent Auditor and the Conduct of an Audit in Accordance With Generally Accepted Auditing Standards* (AICPA, *Professional Standards*). Other auditing publications have no authoritative status; however, they may help the auditor understand and apply generally accepted auditing standards.

In applying the auditing guidance included in an other auditing publication, the auditor should, using professional judgment, assess the relevance and appropriateness of such guidance to the circumstances of the audit. The auditing guidance in this document has been reviewed by the AICPA Audit and Attest Standards staff and published by the AICPA and is presumed to be appropriate. This document has not been approved, disapproved, or otherwise acted on by a senior technical committee of the AICPA.

Potential Benefits of Increased Use of ADAs

Audit data analytics (ADA or ADAs) are defined as "...the science and art of discovering and analyzing patterns, identifying anomalies, and extracting other useful information in data underlying or related to the subject matter of an audit through analysis, modeling, and visualization for the purpose of planning or performing the audit."[1]

In short, ADAs are techniques that can be used to perform various audit procedures, including elements of risk assessment, tests of controls, substantive procedures (that is, tests of details or substantive analytical procedures), or concluding audit procedures. ADAs and analytical procedures are interrelated, but not all ADAs are analytical procedures. Analytical procedures required by generally accepted auditing standards (GAAS) are addressed in AU-C section 520, *Analytical Procedures* (AICPA, *Professional Standards*), and in AICPA Audit Guide *Analytical Procedures*. (Note that Audit Guide *Analytical Procedures* is an *interpretive publication* as defined in AU-C section 200 and is authoritative.) However, GAAS does not require or reference the application of ADAs.

A key objective of this publication is to introduce auditors who are not familiar with ADAs to basic concepts underlying their use and provide examples of how they might be used in practice. Future editions of this publication, or other guidance, will likely be published to reflect ongoing developments in the use of data analytics in financial statement audits.

---

[1] Byrnes, Paul; Criste, Tom; Stewart, Trevor; and Vasarhelyi, Miklos. "Reimagining Auditing in a Wired World." Accessed April 30, 2017, www.aicpa.org/interestareas/frc/assuranceadvisoryservices/downloadabledocuments/whitepaper_blue_sky_scenario-pinkbook.pdf.

Audits of the financial statements of entities of all types and sizes are now being performed in an environment where there is pervasive use of information technology. In this context, increased use of ADAs is likely to be important to maintaining and enhancing the relevance and value of the financial statement audit. Benefits of making more use of ADAs include the following:

- *Improved understanding of an entity's operations and associated risks, including the risk of fraud.* The use of ADAs can help auditors obtain a deeper understanding of the entity under audit. A better understanding of the entity can help the auditor identify either previously unidentified risks or areas where the risk is higher than initially assessed, thereby enabling the auditor to better focus the audit procedures accordingly. Through a better understanding of an entity's operations, the auditor is also better equipped to identify where or how fraud may be perpetrated.

- *Increased potential for detecting material misstatements.* Auditors often use sampling for tests of controls and substantive procedures. ADAs may be used to efficiently and effectively examine aspects of 100 percent of items in a population of relevant data at various levels of aggregation. This may enable auditors to reduce the use of sampling and thereby more effectively manage sampling risk (that is, the risk that the auditor's conclusion based on a sample may be different from the conclusion if the entire population were subjected to the same audit procedure).[2] In addition, use of ADAs, in some cases, may enable the auditor to more effectively and efficiently consider various aspects of the reliability of data. However, sampling would still remain as a useful audit technique in many circumstances.

- *Improved communications with those charged with governance of audited entities.* As a result of the matters noted in the preceding bullet points, an auditor's use of ADAs may provide a greater breadth and depth of useful insights into matters of concern to those charged with governance.[3] When using ADAs, auditors often may be able to more efficiently and effectively describe matters identified by the audit, for example, by using graphics developed in performing the ADAs. Discussions with those charged with governance can then focus more productively on the reasons why certain matters occurred and the possible implications for control, financial reporting, or governance processes.

Recognition

The AICPA gratefully acknowledges the following members of the AICPA Audit Data Analytics Task Force and others who reviewed or otherwise contributed to the development of this publication.

---

[2] This definition of *sampling risk* is set out in paragraph .05 of AU-C section 530, *Audit Sampling* (AICPA, *Professional Standards*).

[3] Paragraph .16 of AU-C section 260, *The Auditor's Communication With Those Charged With Governance* (AICPA, *Professional Standards*), requires the auditor to communicate with those charged with governance regarding specific matters and, as well, "other matters, if any arising from the audit that, in the auditor's professional judgment, are significant to the oversight of the financial reporting process."

Audit Data Analytics Working Group (2015–2017)

Brian P. Collins, *Chair*
Efrim Boritz
Eric E. Cohen
Evan DeFord
Nicole Deschamps
Brian Foster
Katie Greehan
Jason Guthrie
Kristine Hasenstab
Daniel Hevia
Qi Liu
Kevin Macfee
Brian Miller
Nicole Oberst
Trevor Stewart
Miklos A. Vasarhelyi
Brian Wolohan
Michael Yates
Juli-ann Gorgi, *Observer*
Kaylynn Pippo, *Observer*

The AICPA also thanks Gregory P. Shields for his invaluable assistance in authoring this publication and Trevor Stewart for the development of the regression analysis example. Thanks also to those ASB members and their firms who read the draft publication and provided valuable input on how to make this a better publication.

AICPA Staff

Charles E. Landes
Vice President
Professional Standards Team

Amy Pawlicki
Vice President
Assurance and Advisory Innovation

Ami Beers
Director
Assurance & Advisory Services—Corporate Reporting

Ahava Goldman
Associate Director
Audit & Attest Standards

Dorothy McQuilken
Senior Manager
Audit Data Analytics & ERM

AICPA.org Website

The AICPA encourages you to visit the website at www.aicpa.org and the Financial Reporting Center at www.aicpa.org/frc. The Financial Reporting Center supports members in the execution of high-quality financial reporting. Whether you are a financial statement preparer or a member in public practice, this center provides exclusive member-only resources for the entire financial reporting process and provides timely and relevant news, guidance, and examples supporting the financial reporting process. Another important focus of the Financial Reporting Center is keeping those in public practice up to date on issues pertaining to preparation, compilation, review, audit, attestation, assurance, and advisory engagements. Certain content on the AICPA's websites referenced in this publication may be restricted to AICPA members only.

TABLE OF CONTENTS

Chapter 1

Introduction

Scan this QR code with your phone to learn more about audit data analytics and some of the projects that the Association is working on in this area. Free QR code readers are available in your phone's app store.

Objectives of This Guide

1.01 This guide is intended to do the following:

- Assist auditors in applying audit data analytics (ADAs) in performing audit engagements.

  — ADAs are *"the science and art of discovering and analyzing patterns, identifying anomalies, and extracting other useful information in data underlying or related to the subject matter of an audit through analysis, modeling, and visualization for the purpose of planning or performing the audit."*[1]

  — For the purposes of this guide, "an ADA" or "ADAs" are data analytic techniques that can be used to perform risk assessment, tests of controls, substantive procedures (that is, tests of details or substantive analytical procedures), or concluding audit procedures.

The profession needs to transition to increased use of ADAs to provide an opportunity to enhance audit quality, in particular, to respond to a business environment characterized by pervasive use of IT, increased availability of large amounts of data, and increased use of IT-based data analytic tools and techniques by audited entities of all types and sizes.

1.02 Specific objectives of this guide include the following:

- Make auditors aware of how various ADAs may be efficiently and effectively used in each phase of a financial statement audit

---

[1] Byrnes, Paul; Criste, Tom; Stewart, Trevor; and Vasarhelyi, Miklos. "Reimagining Auditing in a Wired World." Accessed April 30, 2017, www.aicpa.org/interestareas/frc/assuranceadvisoryservices/downloadabledocuments/whitepaper_blue_sky_scenario-pinkbook.pdf.

performed in accordance with generally accepted auditing standards (GAAS)

- Helping auditors identify and address matters that they may encounter in deciding whether and, if so, how to use ADAs

Structure, Form, and Content of This Guide

1.03 This chapter provides an overview of topics related to planning and performing ADAs. Subsequent chapters provide more detail on some of these topics as well as examples to illustrate the application of concepts described in this chapter.

1.04 In addition to matters related to the objectives, structure, format, and content of the guide, this chapter provides an overview of the following:

- Relationships among analytical procedures, computer-assisted audit techniques (CAATs) and ADAs
- The importance of specifying and documenting the purpose and nature of the procedure being performed
- An overview of key matters underlying the selection and performance of ADAs, including
  - use of graphics and tables (visualization),
  - access and preparing data to enable their use for purposes of the ADA,
  - relevance and reliability of data,
  - addressing circumstances in which an ADA identifies items, including a large number of items, for further consideration, and
  - documenting the results of an ADA

1.05 Chapters 2–4 describe aspects of a suggested five-step process that an auditor might use for planning, performing, and evaluating the results of an ADA performed in various phases of an audit.

1.06 Chapter 2 discusses the use of ADAs in performing risk assessment procedures. There is also a brief discussion of the use of ADAs in helping the auditor form an overall conclusion. Appendix A provides the following examples:

- Example 2-1—Non-Statistical Trend Analysis of Sales Revenue
- Example 2-2—Preliminary General Ledger Account Balance Analysis
- Example 2-3—Analysis of Customer Accounts Receivable Churn
- Example 2-4—Quantity and Pricing Analysis of Sales Revenue
- Example 2-5—Process Mining—Revenue Process From Sales Order to Sales Invoice

1.07 Chapter 3 discusses the use of ADAs in the performance of substantive analytical procedures in accordance with AU-C section 520, *Analytical Procedures*. Appendix B provides two examples:

- Example 3-1—Non-Statistical Predictive Model for Rental Revenue

- Example 3-2—Regression Analysis of Revenue From Sales of Steam

1.08 Chapter 4 discusses the potential use of ADAs in tests of details. Appendix C provides two examples:

- Example 4-1—Cash Receipt to Sales Invoice Matching Procedure

- Example 4-2—Three-Way Match of Sales Invoices, Shipping Documents, and a Master Price List

1.09 This guide does not discuss the use of ADAs in performing tests of controls. Before guidance can be developed, more information is needed. Auditors are encouraged to explore these matters further.

1.10 In addition to the appendixes discussed previously, appendix D, "Matters to Consider Regarding the Reliability of Data," provides guidance with respect to the important topic of data reliability in the context of performing data analytic techniques.

1.11 QC section 10, *A Firm's System of Quality Control* (AICPA, *Professional Standards*), sets out the firm's responsibilities to establish and maintain its system of quality control for audit engagements and to establish policies and procedures designed to provide it with reasonable assurance that the firm and its personnel comply with relevant ethical requirements, including those pertaining to independence and so on. Certain aspects regarding the use of ADAs may need to be addressed by a firm's quality control policies and procedures, such as the assignment of engagement teams with appropriate competencies and the use of appropriate tools and software. Discussion of these matters is beyond the scope of this guide.

Considerations Regarding Examples in This Guide and Other Matters

1.12 This guide provides numerous examples that illustrate the use of ADAs in a financial statement audit. To avoid misinterpreting the application of examples, it is important to consider the following caveats:

- This guide is an *other auditing publication* as defined in AU-C section 200, *Overall Objectives of the Independent Auditor and the Conduct of an Audit in Accordance with Generally Accepted Auditing Standards*, and discusses how an auditor might apply ADAs in the performance of an audit and does not result in any requirements beyond those included in GAAS. For example, this guide cannot require the auditor to perform a procedure when such performance is not required by GAAS.

- No auditor decision described in an example, or any percentage or amount used in an example, is meant to have general applicability. Auditors in circumstances similar to those noted in the examples often might come to different conclusions and make different decisions based on the specific facts and circumstances and use of their own professional judgment.

1.13 This guide also makes references to the "year under audit" and "year end." The guidance would also apply to audits of financial statements covering different periods.

Relationship Between ADAs, CAATs, and Analytical Procedures

1.14 ADAs are defined in paragraph 1.01 and may be used throughout the audit, as noted in exhibit 1-1. Although ADAs are not specifically referred to in GAAS, there are references to computer-assisted audit techniques (CAATs). Many similarities can be drawn between ADAs and CAATs. ADAs could be applied manually to discover and analyze patterns, identify anomalies, and extract other useful information in data. However, in practice, they would seldom be performed without using a computer. In that regard, ADAs might be viewed as an evolutionary form of CAATS that have, for example, enabled the auditor to make more effective use of data visualization techniques and help achieve a broader range of audit objectives.

Exhibit 1-1

Potential Use of ADAs Throughout the Audit

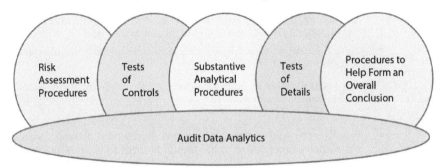

1.15 ADAs, as defined in paragraph 1.01, are techniques that can be used in the performance of analytical procedures. For the purposes of GAAS, analytical procedures are

> [e]valuations of financial information through analysis of plausible relationships among both financial and nonfinancial data. Analytical procedures also encompass such investigation, as is necessary, of identified fluctuations or relationships that are inconsistent with other relevant information or that differ from expected values by a significant amount.[2]

1.16 As can be seen from the respective definitions, ADAs are techniques that can be used to perform a wide variety of audit procedures, including analytic procedures.

Exercising Professional Judgment and Maintaining Professional Skepticism

1.17 GAAS requires the auditor to plan and perform the audit with professional skepticism and exercise professional judgment.[3] When performing an audit procedure, the auditor applies professional judgment and skepticism to help reduce, for example, the risks of the following:

- Using inappropriate assumptions in planning the procedures and evaluating the results obtained
- Overlooking unusual circumstances
- Over-generalizing in drawing conclusions

Considerations in Determining Which ADA to Use to Meet the Objective of the Audit Procedure

1.18 The examples in this guide illustrate various ADAs that an auditor may consider performing as part of the audit process to meet specific audit

---

[2] See paragraph .04 of AU-C section 520, *Analytical Procedures*. All AU-C sections referenced in this guide can be found in AICPA *Professional Standards*.

[3] Paragraphs .17–.18 of AU-C section 200, *Overall Objectives of the Independent Auditor and the Conduct of an Audit in Accordance With Generally Accepted Auditing Standards*.

objectives. Various tools and methods also need to be considered. Note the following for the purposes of this guide:

- *Techniques* are variations in the way an ADA might be applied. These may include, for example, the way in which data is accessed, organized, analyzed, and the results communicated

- *Tools* include, when applicable, the software (or particular aspects of software) that is used

1.19 Examples of matters an auditor may consider in determining which ADA to use, and the methods and tools to use in applying it, include the following:

- Whether the ADA is to be used in risk assessment, test of controls, substantive procedures, or in helping to form an overall audit conclusion

- The nature and extent of the account balances, classes of transactions, and related assertions for which the ADA is being used

- The persuasiveness of the audit evidence, including, where applicable, the level of precision the ADA is intended to provide

- The types of risk of material misstatement it is expected to respond to when used in a substantive procedure

- Whether the ADA is intended to be focused on any combination, or all, of the following:

  — Organizing data into some form of hierarchy to enable further analysis (for example, sorting or classification)

  — Determining the key attributes of specified types of accounts or classes of transactions

  — Searching for data with specified characteristics

  — Developing an estimate of a value or another attribute

  — Identifying data that has attributes that are outside of specified ranges (for example, values or frequencies of occurrence that are significantly higher or lower than would normally be expected in the circumstances)

  — Identifying data having similar attributes when that would not normally be expected in the circumstances

  — Determining whether there are relationships (for example, correlations or causal relationships) among variables

Using Graphics and Tables (Visualization)

1.20 Another key consideration in helping to achieve the objective of an ADA is the determination of the nature and extent of the use of visualization techniques. The term *visualization* may refer to the use of various types of graphics (for example, charts, scatter diagrams, trend lines), tables, or combinations thereof in formats such as dashboards.[4] In this guide, the discussion is

---

[4] A *dashboard* is a series of related graphics or visualizations that the auditor may use to analyze the underlying data, similar in concept to speedometers, odometers, and gas gauges used on dashboards of automobiles.

limited to graphics and tables. The auditor might, for example, use graphics as part of an ADA to help quickly identify matters that are likely to be significant to performing and reaching conclusions from the ADA. Conversely, an effective graphic might help the auditor conclude that there are no matters arising from the ADA that need particular auditor attention.

1.21 It is a matter of professional judgment for the auditor to decide whether to use some form of graphic or table as part of performing an ADA and, if so, what its form and content might be.

1.22 Often, an effective approach might be to use both a table and one or more graphics. For example, a software pivot table tool can be used to automatically sort, count, total, or perform other functions on data contained in one table or spreadsheet and display the results in a summarized format in a second table (that is, the pivot table). A pivot chart generated by the software may be used to show a graphic of the information in the pivot table in a format recommended by the software.

1.23 As with the pivot table or pivot chart tool referred to in paragraph 1.22, software used in performing an ADA often will contain an option to use a graphic format (for example, a trend line, bar chart, histogram, pie chart, or scatterplot) recommended by the software. The recommendation will be based on aspects of the data type. The software-recommended format can be a useful starting point in determining what graphics may work well in the circumstances. Typically, there will be numerous options (for example, color, size, angle, proportions, and axis attributes) for customizing how the information will be displayed, even within a particular format. The auditor might evaluate the format of the graphic recommended by the software and use professional judgment in deciding whether it is appropriate. Sometimes, an auditor experienced with graphics is able to develop a more effective graphic than that generated using preset options in the software.

Graphics Often Linked With Particular ADAs

1.24 Some graphic formats often are closely linked to the nature of the ADA being performed. For example, for a regression analysis, graphics often may include a scatterplot (showing the set of data points for two variables) and a trend line (that is, the line of best fit for the points in the scatterplot). The graphic might be used to help clearly show the relationship between the dependent and independent variables. Using software, it is possible to develop more complex graphics, if desired. Appendix B shows various graphics that are likely to be effective when using regression analysis.

Matters to Consider Regarding Graphic Design

1.25 If a graph, trend line, or other graphic is improperly designed, the result may be that the auditor fails to identify an important matter that requires additional focus. On the other hand, an improperly designed graphic might lead the auditor to identify a matter for follow-up work when, in fact, no further work is warranted. Three examples of matters to consider in designing graphics in an auditing context are set out in exhibits 1-2 through 1-4.

Exhibit 1-2

Graphics Regarding Journal Entries

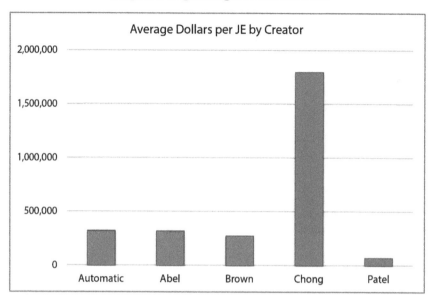

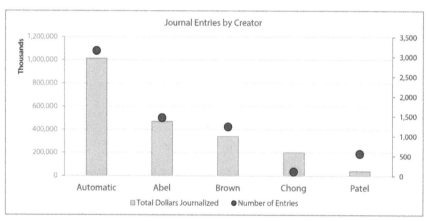

Level of Detail in a Graphic

1.26 ADAs are often used to help auditors address high volumes of complex data. It may sometimes be tempting to try to include as much information as possible within one graphic. However, that may defeat the purpose of using the graphic to help the auditor readily identify and focus on an area warranting further attention. A general principle to consider is that if a graphic requires an explanation regarding what it is meant to convey, then it is not likely an effective graphic. On the other hand, a graphic may have too little detail. Exhibit 1-2 provides an example of how a graphic may provide more information in a clear way without an overwhelming amount of detail. In this case, the first graphic shows only average dollars per journal entry by preparer. The second provides different information (that is, total dollar value and total number of entries by preparer). This is potentially useful without adding a lot of complexity. For example, the graphic might show that a creator has made only a few journal entries, but they have a high dollar value. Such entries may be unusual in the circumstances of the particular audit, and the auditor may identify the entries for testing.

Exhibit 1-3

Effects on Graphic of Changes in Vertical Axis Scale

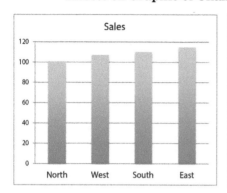
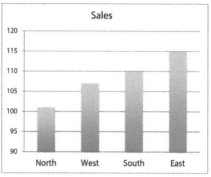

Scaling of Axes on a Graph

1.27 The information conveyed by a graphic can be significantly affected by the scaling of the vertical or horizontal axis. For example, the relative lengths of bars in a bar chart or the steepness of the slope of a trend line (either up or down) may be used to indicate the significance of differences in variables. However, these, and other aspects of graphics, can be very different depending on the scales of the axes used. Exhibit 1-3 shows two graphics that give significantly different impressions using the same data set.

Exhibit 1-4

Graphics With Different Emphasis Based on Same Underlying Data

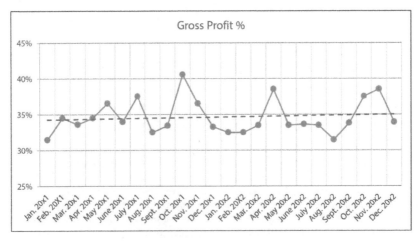

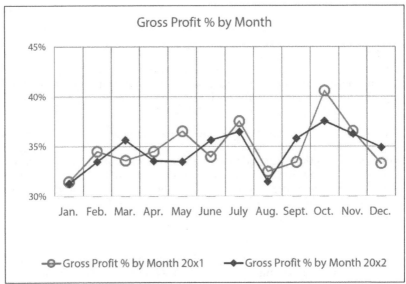

Primary Focus of a Graphic

1.28 In exhibit 1-4, the first graphic shows the trend of gross profit percentage by month and its volatility among the various months. It might lead to more in-depth audit work for months with highs and lows that are furthest from the trend line. The second graphic, based on the same data, focuses on comparing each month for the past two years. It shows, for example, that for each quarter end in 20x2 (when the company reports externally), gross profit percentages are higher than those from 20x1. This is the reverse of the relationship in other months. This is not readily apparent from the first graphic but might be a matter warranting follow-up work.

DATA 1.28

Accessing and Preparing Data for Purposes of an ADA

1.29 These are two key issues that the auditor may face in accessing data:

- Ability to obtain or access the data in a format that the auditor can readily use

- The audited entity's concerns about the auditor's ability to maintain data security and integrity

1.30 The auditor may also encounter issues in preparing the data as discussed in paragraphs 1.36–1.37.

Accessing Data in a Format the Auditor Can Use

1.31 The information systems used by audited entities have different platforms (that is, hardware, software, database, and network components). There also are various procedures for combining those components to capture, process, store data, and report information. Even within the same entity, there may be various systems. For example, the entity may store data in an enterprise resource planning (ERP) system, one or more legacy systems, or in an external data repository, including internet-based repositories. Auditors have to address this variety of systems in accessing data.

1.32 In some cases, auditors may be able to use data-import functions commonly available in business software. However, audit software (acquired from a third-party supplier or developed in-house) may be more efficient and effective in accessing data. For example, such software may be capable of importing data from many types of sources, either directly from accounting software or by using a connector (that is, a software interface) when accessing data in an ERP system.

1.33 However, the format of the entity's data may present challenges. Currently, no commonly used standardized data format exists that would allow auditors to more efficiently and effectively access data of all entities. Possible solutions to this issue are evolving. For example, the AICPA has developed and continues to expand voluntary, uniform AICPA Audit Data Standards. These standards may help to identify key information needed for audits and provide a common framework that includes

- data file and data field definitions and technical specifications, and

- supplemental questions and data preparation routines to help auditors better understand the data and assess its integrity.[5]

Maintaining Data Security, Confidentiality, and Integrity

1.34 Because entities need to maintain the integrity and security of their data, the auditor often may encounter resistance from entities to having their data accessed by the auditor's systems. Management may have concerns that analyses performed by auditors may corrupt or change the data. In addition, some entities may worry that data security breaches (that is, unauthorized access by third parties to their data) may result in loss of confidentiality (or for

---

[5] The AICPA Audit Data Standards, including *Base Standard, General Ledger Standard* and standards for various sub-ledgers, can be found on the AICPA website at aicpa.org.

some types of data, privacy) when auditors have imported company data to the auditor's systems.

1.35 The auditor may consider in advance how to effectively respond to concerns raised by entities. For example, the auditor may be able to describe how the system complies with principles and criteria used in evaluating controls relevant to the integrity and security of data.

Preparing the Data for Use

1.36 In many cases, preparation (or cleansing or scrubbing) of the entity's data may be needed before a meaningful analysis of the data can be undertaken. Data preparation is the process of identifying data errors of which there are many types. For example, some fields that should always contain data may have none; fields that should contain dates may have letters or other types of numbers; or there may be fields that contain data outside preset acceptable minimum or maximum acceptable values. As another example, data from different systems may vary in organization within a field. Some examples are dates being in a month-day-year versus a day-month-year format and numbers having different decimal indicators, such as the period or full stop (.) in the United Sates and the comma (,) in Europe (for example, the European "," vs. the United States ".").

1.37 Some data error issues may be relatively easy to resolve. However, the frequency and nature of matters identified may call into question whether the quality of data is appropriate for use by the auditor. These matters may indicate, for example, that controls over the data are not operating effectively. In rare cases, indications may be that the data will not be auditable until the entity undertakes an investigation to determine the root causes of the issues and takes further appropriate actions to correct the records.

Relevance and Reliability of Data

1.38 The auditor considers whether data is relevant and sufficiently reliable to meet the objectives of the procedure. Various paragraphs in GAAS refer to this interconnection among relevance and reliability. Examples include the following:

- Paragraph .A20 of AU-C section 330, *Performing Audit Procedures in Response to Assessed Risks and Evaluating the Audit Evidence Obtained*, states that when obtaining more persuasive audit evidence because of a higher assessment of risk, the auditor may increase the quantity of the evidence or obtain evidence that is more relevant or reliable (for example, by placing more emphasis on obtaining third party evidence or by obtaining corroborating evidence from a number of independent sources).

- Paragraph .05b of AU-C section 520 requires the auditor to evaluate the reliability of data from which the auditor's expectation of recorded amounts or ratios is developed, taking into account the source, comparability, and nature and relevance of information available and controls over preparation. Paragraph .A8c refers to the availability and reliability of the data used to develop the expectation. In addition, paragraph .A17 discusses what is relevant when determining whether data is reliable for purposes of designing substantive analytical procedures and refers in item (c) to the relevance of information available.

- Paragraph .A75 of AU-C section 330 refers to a number of factors that influence the auditor's professional judgment about what constitutes sufficient appropriate audit evidence. One factor noted is the source and reliability of available information.

Data Characteristics That May Affect Relevance and Reliability of Data

1.39 Exhibit 1-5 shows data characteristics that may affect, to varying degrees, the relevance and reliability of data. For example, whether the source of the data is internal or external is likely to be a significant factor affecting the auditor's ability to assess reliability of the data. The significance of other characteristics (such as whether data is historic, forward-looking, or time-sensitive) is likely to be more dependent on the particular circumstances in which the procedure is being used. The examples in appendix D illustrate how some of these characteristics might affect the auditor's ability to assess the reliability of the data, as well as the nature and extent of procedures to be performed on the data in order to establish a basis for reliance upon it.

Exhibit 1-5

Examples of Data Characteristics That May Affect Data Relevance and Reliability

NATURE

- Financial, nonfinancial
- Accounting process and control-related
- Product and service categories
- Demographic
- Economic
- Geographic
- Business sector
- Regulatory
- Historic
- Forward-looking
- Time-sensitive
- Metadata (for example, file labels, record formats, access and other authorization codes)
- Raw situational data (for example, customer activity from customer relationship management system)
- Descriptive information (for example, quality metrics)
- Summarized data (for example, research reports)

SOURCES

- Controlled by the accounting department of the audited entity (in-house records or stored externally (for example, in the cloud)
- Controlled by persons outside of the accounting department of the audited entity (with various possible storage media, as noted in the previous list item)
- External to, and not controlled by, the audited entity

FORMAT

- Numerical (for example, quantity, currency), text, symbols, other characters
- Structured (for example, data in a fixed field within a record or file)
- Unstructured (for example, text)

TIMING

- Point-in-time, period of time
- Rate of change (time lags, continuity)

EXTENT

- Volume
- Scope (variety of subject matters and sources)

(continued)

**Examples of Data Characteristics That May Affect Data Relevance
and Reliability**—*continued*

LEVEL OF AGGREGATION

- Financial statement item, account balance, component of an account balance
- Annual, monthy, daily, hourly, some smaller timing frequency
- Consolidated, segmented (for example, by division, location)
- Database files, tables, and fields

Relevance of Data

1.40 Paragraph .A28 of AU-C section 500, *Audit Evidence*, states that relevance relates to the logical connection with, or bearing upon, the purpose of the audit procedure and, when appropriate, the assertion under consideration. The relevance of information used as audit evidence may be affected, for example, by the direction of testing (that is, whether the auditor is testing for overstatements or understatements).

1.41 In addition, other paragraphs in AU-C section 500 state the following regarding relevance:

- A given set of audit procedures may provide audit evidence that is relevant to certain assertions but not others.[6]

- Designing tests of controls to obtain relevant audit evidence includes identifying conditions (characteristics or attributes) that indicate performance of a control and identifying deviation conditions that indicate departures from adequate performance.[7]

- Designing substantive procedures includes identifying conditions relevant to the purpose of the test that constitute a misstatement in the relevant assertion.[8]

Reliability of Data

1.42 The auditor considers the accuracy and completeness of data when evaluating its reliability, taking into account, for example, the objectives of the procedures for which the data is being used.

1.43 As noted previously, data reliability may be affected by many factors as well as by the interrelationships among those factors. Appendix D to this guide sets out matters auditors may wish to consider in assessing whether data is sufficiently reliable.

1.44 Appendix D covers the following in detail:

- Extracts from GAAS that discuss aspects of data reliability. These include quotes from the following:

---

[6] Paragraph .A29 of AU-C section 500, *Audit Evidence*.
[7] Paragraph .A30 of AU-C section 500.
[8] Paragraph .A31 of AU-C section 500.

— AU-C section 200 and AU-C section 315, *Understanding the Entity and Its Environment and Assessing the Risks of Material Misstatement*, regarding the relationships between audit evidence, information and data, and how the use of IT results in benefits and risks may affect the reliability of data

— AU-C section 500 regarding how the auditor may take different approaches to address matters related to the reliability of data depending on, for example, whether the data is from an external or internal source and how audit evidence itself is influenced by its source, nature, and the circumstances under which it is obtained, including the controls over its preparation and maintenance, when relevant

— AU-C section 520, including the requirement for the auditor to evaluate the reliability of data (internal or external) from which the auditor's expectation of recorded amounts or ratios is developed

— AU-C section 540, *Auditing Accounting Estimates, Including Fair Value Accounting Estimates, and Related Disclosures*, regarding matters related to data reliability when auditing an accounting estimate, including the effect of data reliability on measurement uncertainty

● Examples of approaches an auditor might use in determining whether data is sufficiently reliable, taking into account in each example:

— The circumstances in which the analytical procedure or ADA is being performed (for example, as a risk assessment procedure, as a test of controls, as a substantive analytical procedure, or a test of details) and the auditor's objective in performing it

— The risk assessment associated with the account or assertion(s) being audited

— The extent of the other audit procedures being performed on the account or assertion(s)

— The nature of the data

— The source of the data

— The process used to produce the data

— Procedures regarding data reliability that an auditor may consider performing

Possible Sequence of Procedures Regarding Data Relevance and Reliability

1.45 No specific sequence of audit steps exists to address relevance and reliability. However, performing steps in the following order may help to achieve the objective of the procedure:

1. Consider what data is likely to be most relevant to performing the ADA effectively and efficiently.

2. Determine whether all the data considered most relevant is readily available. If not, determine what steps may be viable to obtain access to that data. The result may be, for example, that only some of the most relevant data is available. In that case, the auditor considers whether there is enough data with sufficient relevance to provide useful audit evidence.

3. If data of sufficient relevance is available, the auditor considers, on a preliminary basis, whether that data is likely to have sufficient reliability for the purposes of the ADA. Appendix D to this guide discusses the reliability of data.

Addressing Circumstances in Which an ADA Identifies a Large Number of Items for Further Consideration

1.46 When ADAs involve 100 percent of items in sizeable populations, the auditor may initially identify a large number of items requiring some form of auditor consideration to ensure that risk is sufficiently low. In some cases, items initially identified using an ADA may, in fact, represent a previously unidentified risk or a higher level of risk of material misstatement than initially assessed, control deficiencies, or misstatements. In other cases, some or all the items identified using the ADA may not, in fact, represent those types of matters (that is, those items may be what are sometimes called "false positives"). In determining whether the items identified warrant an audit response, further attention may not necessarily involve the performance of an investigation of each individual item identified. For example, the auditor's response might include one or more of the following:

- More clearly defining the characteristics of the data that are likely to be indicative of matters that require an audit response and then re-applying the ADA using these more clearly defined characteristics.

- Identifying subgroups within the population of items that initially appear to warrant further attention and designing and performing additional procedures that may effectively and efficiently be applied to each subgroup. That further analysis might, for example, provide evidence that a subgroup does not represent a risk of material misstatement, control deficiencies, or misstatements. On the other hand, the follow-up analysis might indicate that the items in a subgroup require further response from the auditor. The nature, timing, and extent of additional procedures required would take into account the relevant characteristics of the items in the subgroup.

- Applying a different ADA, or another procedure, that might more clearly identify those items that represent a risk of material misstatement, control deficiencies, or misstatements.

1.47 Appendixes A, B, and C provide examples to illustrate the application of the process in paragraph 1.46.

Documenting the Procedures

GAAS Requirements Regarding Documentation

1.48 Paragraph .08 of AU-C section 230, *Audit Documentation*, states that the auditor should prepare audit documentation that is sufficient to enable an experienced auditor, having no previous connection with the audit, to understand the following:

    a. The nature, timing, and extent of the audit procedures performed to comply with GAAS and applicable legal and regulatory requirements

    b. The results of the audit procedures performed, and the audit evidence obtained

    c. Significant findings or issues arising during the audit, the conclusions reached thereon, and significant professional judgments made in reaching those conclusions[9]

1.49 Paragraph .09 of AU-C section 230 states that in documenting the nature, timing, and extent of audit procedures performed, the auditor should record the following:

    a. The identifying characteristics of the specific items or matters tested

    b. Who performed the audit work and the date such work was completed

    c. Who reviewed the audit work performed and the date and extent of such review

1.50 As noted in paragraph .A14 of AU-C section 230, identifying characteristics will vary with the nature of the audit procedure and the item or matter tested. Consistent with that paragraph, for an ADA, the auditor may record the scope of the procedure and identify the population analyzed or tested. GAAS do not require (nor, in many cases, is it practicable) to include in the audit file, or incorporate by reference, all the data analyzed or tested using an audit procedure.

1.51 Consistent with paragraph 1.48, the documentation may include the following:

- Objectives of the procedure
- Risks of material misstatement that the procedure intended to address at the financial statement level or at the assertion level
- The sources of the underlying data and how it was determined to be sufficient and appropriate (as necessary in the context of the nature and objectives of the ADA being performed)
- The ADA and related tools and techniques used
- The tables or graphics used, including how they were generated
- The steps taken to access data, including the system accessed and, when applicable, how the data was extracted and transformed for audit use

---

[9] Paragraph .06 of AU-C section 230, *Audit Documentation*, defines *experienced auditor*.

       DATA 1.51

- The evaluation of matters identified as a result of applying the ADA and actions taken regarding those matters
- The identifying characteristics of the specific items or matters tested
- The individual who performed the audit work and the date such work was completed
- The individual who reviewed the audit work performed and the date and extent of such review

1.52 Paragraph .08 of AU-C section 520 contains documentation requirements specific to substantive analytical procedures. These are noted in paragraph 3.63 of this guide.

Screenshots of Graphics

1.53 When performing an ADA, graphics will often be generated, or customized by the auditor, to help provide insights into matters the auditor identifies. The underlying data from the graphic will not generally be included in the audit documentation. In that case, screenshots of the relevant graphics will be included in the auditor's documentation because the graphic would no longer be directly linked to the data sets to which they relate. However, only those graphics necessary to support the auditor's work would need to be retained. For example, there would be no need to retain a screenshot showing the activity for all accounts when the ADA is targeted at auditing revenue. The graphics retained would be those related to the audit of revenues.

Documenting Process to Address a Large Number of Items Warranting Further Consideration

1.54 Chapters 2 and 4 of this guide discuss circumstances when, as a result of performing an ADA, a large number of items are identified that warrant a response from the auditor. The auditor would document, for example, the process used for grouping and filtering items with common characteristics and determining the cause of the items in each group.

1.55 It is neither necessary nor practicable for the auditor to document every matter considered or professional judgment made in an audit.[10] If large numbers of items warranting an auditor response are identified, the auditor may, for example, document how the items were filtered and grouped (providing a summary of the key characteristics and frequency of occurrence of the items identified) and the procedures performed to address and evaluate each common group of items.

1.56 All misstatements identified as a result of an ADA, other than those that are clearly trivial, should be documented.[11]

---

[10] Paragraph .A9 of AU-C section 230.

[11] Paragraph .12 of AU-C section 450, *Evaluation of Misstatements Identified During the Audit.*

Chapter 2

Using ADAs in Performing Risk Assessment Procedures and in Procedures to Assist When Forming an Overall Conclusion

Matters Covered in This Chapter

2.01 This chapter discusses the use of ADAs in performing

- risk assessment procedures (paragraphs 2.04–2.26) and
- procedures to assist the auditor when forming an overall conclusion about whether the financial statements are consistent with the auditor's understanding of the entity (paragraphs 2.27–2.29).

2.02 The matters discussed in this chapter are based on concepts introduced in chapter 1. Paragraph 1.17 emphasizes the need for the auditor to exercise professional judgment and professional skepticism in planning, performing, and evaluating the results of an audit procedure.

2.03 Appendix A sets out the following examples of the use of ADAs in performing risk assessment procedures.

- Example 2-1—Non-Statistical Trend Analysis of Sales Revenue
- Example 2-2—Preliminary General Ledger Account Balance Analysis
- Example 2-3—Analysis of Customer Accounts Receivable Churn
- Example 2-4—Quantity and Pricing Analysis of Sales Revenue
- Example 2-5—Process Mining—Revenue Process From Sales Order to Sales Invoice

Specific Generally Accepted Auditing Standards Relevant to Use of ADAs in Performing Risk Assessment Procedures

Definition of *Risk Assessment Procedures*

2.04 *Risk assessment procedures* are "the audit procedures performed to obtain an understanding of the entity and its environment, including the entity's internal control, to identify and assess the risks of material misstatement, whether due to fraud or error, at the financial statement and relevant assertion levels."[1] Therefore, the use of ADAs in performing risk assessment procedures may relate to the identification of risks of material misstatement, the assessment of such risks, or both.

---

[1] See paragraph .04 of AU-C section 315, *Understanding the Entity and Its Environment and Assessing the Risks of Material Misstatement.*

Requirement for Risk Assessment Procedures to Include Analytical Procedures

2.05   Paragraph .06*b* of AU-C section 315, *Understanding the Entity and Its Environment and Assessing the Risks of Material Misstatement*, requires risk assessment procedures to include analytical procedures. Auditors might decide to use ADAs in performing analytical procedures designed to identify and assess risks of material misstatement.

Planning Considerations for Using ADAs in Risk Assessment Procedures

2.06   Paragraph .A2 of AU-C section 300, *Planning an Audit*, states that planning includes the need to consider, prior to the auditor's identification and assessment of the risks of material misstatement, such matters as the following:

- The analytical procedures to be applied as risk assessment procedures
- A general understanding of the legal and regulatory framework applicable to the entity and how the entity is complying with that framework
- The determination of materiality
- The involvement of specialists
- The performance of other risk assessment procedures

Audit Evidence Provided by Risk Assessment Procedures

2.07   Key requirements and guidance related to risk assessment procedures, which may be particularly relevant when ADAs are used in performing these procedures, are set out in the following paragraphs in generally accepted auditing standards (GAAS):

- Paragraph .05 of AU-C section 315 states that the auditor should perform risk assessment procedures to provide a basis for the identification and assessment of risks of material misstatement at the financial statement and relevant assertion levels. However, risk assessment procedures, by themselves, do not provide sufficient appropriate audit evidence on which to base the audit opinion.
- Paragraph .A2 of AU-C section 315 states that information obtained by performing risk assessment procedures and related activities may be used by the auditor as audit evidence to support assessments of the risks of material misstatement. In addition, the auditor may obtain audit evidence about classes of transactions, account balances, or disclosures and relevant assertions and about the operating effectiveness of controls, even though such procedures were not specifically planned as substantive procedures or tests of controls. The auditor also may choose to perform substantive procedures or tests of controls concurrently with risk assessment procedures because it is efficient to do so.
- Paragraph .18 of AU-C section 330, *Performing Audit Procedures in Response to Assessed Risks and Evaluating the Audit Evidence Obtained*, states that irrespective of the assessed risks of material

misstatement, the auditor should design and perform substantive procedures for all relevant assertions related to each material class of transactions, account balance, and disclosure. Paragraph .04 of AU-C section 315 defines a relevant assertion as a financial statement assertion that has a reasonable possibility of containing a misstatement or misstatements that would cause the financial statements to be materially misstated. The determination of whether an assertion is a relevant assertion is made without regard to the effect of internal controls.

Applying Five Basic Steps for an ADA

2.08 Exhibit 2-1 sets out five basic steps and related procedures that may be used in planning, performing, and evaluating the results of an ADA used in identifying and assessing risks of material misstatement and to assist when forming an overall conclusion. An auditor might decide to perform steps and procedures other than those set out in exhibit 2-1 or perform them together or perhaps in a different order.

2.09 The discussion in paragraphs 2.10–2.26 highlights considerations for certain aspects of the steps and procedures set out in exhibit 2-1.

Exhibit 2-1

Five Basic Steps and Related Procedures an Auditor Might Use in Planning, Performing, and Evaluating the Results of an ADA Used in Performing a Risk Assessment Procedure and in Assist When Forming an Overall Conclusion

1. **Plan the ADA.**
   a. Determine the financial statement items or accounts, or disclosures, and related assertions and the nature, timing, and extent of the population to which the ADA will be applied.
   b. Determine the overall purpose of the ADA (for example, whether it is to be used in performing a risk assessment procedure, a test of controls, a substantive analytical procedure, a test of details, or in procedures to help form an overall conclusion from the audit).
   c. Determine the specific objectives of the ADA (within the context of its overall purpose).
   d. Determine the data population to be analyzed or tested using the ADA, including, for planning purposes, preliminary consideration of matters likely to affect the relevance, availability, and reliability of that data.
   e. Select the ADA that is likely best suited for the intended purpose and objectives.
   f. Select the techniques, tools, graphics, and tables to be used.
2. **Access and prepare the data for purposes of the ADA.**
3. **Consider the relevance and reliability of the data used.**
4. **Perform the ADA.**
   a. If the initial results of the ADA indicate that aspects of its design or performance need to be revised, make appropriate revisions and reperform the ADA.
   b. If the auditor concludes that the ADA has been properly designed and performed, and the ADA has identified items that warrant further auditor considerations, plan and perform additional procedures on those items consistent with achieving the purpose and specific objectives of the ADA. (Note: See the flowchart in exhibit 2-2 and supporting material for addressing circumstances when a large number of such items has been identified.)
5. **Evaluate the results and conclude on whether the purpose and specific objectives of performing the ADA have been achieved.**
   a. If the objectives have not been achieved, plan and perform different procedures to achieve those objectives.

Documentation: The auditor should comply with the relevant documentation requirements in GAAS when performing each step and related procedure.

Paragraph .33 of AU-C section 315 sets out requirements regarding the documentation of risk assessment procedures. Paragraphs 1.48–1.56 of this guide discuss matters related to documenting ADAs.

Plan the ADA

Determine the Specific Objectives of the ADA (Within the Context of Its Overall Purpose)

2.10 The objective of an ADA may be to identify and assess a risk of material misstatement for one or more relevant assertions pertaining to a class of transactions or account balances or disclosures, or perhaps to identify a condition or event that indicates the existence of a risk of material misstatement. However, it is also possible that as a result of performing the ADA, the auditor may be able to conclude that a risk does not rise to the level of a risk of material misstatement.

2.11 The specific objectives also may be affected, for example, by the aspects of the entity on which the ADA is focused. Those aspects may include obtaining an understanding of various matters as required by GAAS, such as the following:

- Relevant industry, regulatory, and other external factors
- The nature of the entity, including its operations
- The application of the entity's accounting policies
- The entity's objectives and strategies and those related business risks that may result in risks of material misstatement
- The measurement and review of the entity's financial performance
- Internal control relevant to the audit[2]

2.12 The examples provided in this chapter illustrate the use of ADAs in risk assessment procedures, including specific objectives in performing them.

Consider the Relevance and Reliability of the Data Used

2.13 Paragraphs 1.40–1.45 contain a brief discussion of reliability and relevance of data. Appendix D to this guide discusses in more detail matters regarding the reliability of data and also touches upon the relevance of data. Examples addressing data reliability when performing risk assessment procedures are included.

---

[2] See paragraphs .12–.13 of AU-C section 315.

Exhibit 2-2

Process to Identify and Address Notable Items When Using an ADA in Performing a Risk Assessment Procedure

Perform the ADA to identify or assess risks of material misstatement
(Step 4 in the 5-step ADA process [outlined in exhibit 2-1])

Evaluate whether the ADA has been appropriately planned and performed and, if not, refine and reperform it

When appropriate, use groupings and filtering when a large number of notable items is identified

Determine whether notable items result in any of the following:

- Identification of a previously unidentified risk
- Modification or support for the assessment of risks of material misstatement
- Information to better design or tailor audit procedures to address risk of material misstatement

Perform the ADA

Identifying and Addressing Notable Items

2.14 Using an ADA in performing a risk assessment procedure may result in the identification of one or more notable items. For the purposes of this guide, a *notable item* is an item identified from the population being analyzed that has one or more characteristics that, for the relevant assertions, may do the following:

    a. Be indicative of a risk of material misstatement that

        i. was not previously identified (a new risk) or

        ii. is higher than originally assessed by the auditor

    b. Provide information that is useful in designing or tailoring procedures to address risks of material misstatement

2.15 To address notable items identified, the auditor might follow the process described in exhibit 2-2. Starting at the top of the exhibit, the auditor would initially perform the ADA. Moving to the second box, the auditor would evaluate whether the ADA has been appropriately planned and performed and, if not, refine and reperform it. This is an iterative process, that is, the process of refining and reperforming continues until the auditor decides that either the ADA needs no further improvements to achieve the objectives of the procedure or that a different procedure is needed to achieve those objectives.

2.16 The second box in exhibit 2-2 also indicates that the auditor may decide to use groupings and filtering when a large number of notable items is identified. This process is discussed in paragraphs 2.18–2.26. Again, the auditor refines and reperforms the grouping and filtering process until the auditor decides that the ADA needs no further improvements to achieve the objectives of the procedure or that a different procedure is needed to achieve those objectives.

2.17 An appropriately planned and performed ADA may identify a small number of notable items. The auditor might be able to manually (that is, without further use of a computerized analysis) perform additional risk assessment procedures to obtain more information regarding those items. The additional information obtained might focus on their nature, cause, and what can go wrong at the relevant assertion level. This additional information may help the auditor to determine which notable items identified are likely to represent a new risk or a higher level of risk of material misstatement or to better design and perform procedures to respond to the assessed risks of material misstatement. Further audit procedures (in some cases, tests of controls, and in all cases, substantive procedures for relevant assertions) would be performed that are responsive to the assessed risks of material misstatement for the notable item or items.

2.18 The auditor may encounter circumstances in which a large number of notable items is identified as a result of using an ADA in performing a risk assessment procedure. For the purposes of this guide, a large number of notable items may mean, for example, that the number is not practicable for the auditor to address the items manually. For some audits, notable items could number in the hundreds or even thousands for audits of very large organizations. Further use of an ADA is likely required to address the notable items identified.

2.19 As noted in exhibit 2-2, the auditor would first evaluate whether the ADA has been appropriately planned and performed and, if not, refine and reperform it. The auditor might also decide to apply a grouping and filtering process when, for example, a large number of notable items identified have many diverse characteristics. A grouping and filtering process could be used as follows:

a. To identify characteristics common to groups of notable items, focusing on their nature, cause, and what can go wrong at the relevant assertion level.

b. For each group identified in step a, sort the notable items into one of the following two groups:

i. Items requiring no further consideration to identify new or higher risks (sometimes called "false positives")

ii. Items requiring a further consideration from the auditor to identify new or higher risks.

c. Further analyze the characteristics of the items in bii to help identify and sort those notable items into three subgroups:

    i. Those indicating one or more risks of material misstatement of which the auditor was not previously aware (new risks)

    ii. Those indicating a higher level of risk of material misstatement than previously identified

    iii. Those that do not indicate new or higher levels of risk of material misstatement

2.20 For any of the groups in paragraph 2.19, the auditor might also obtain information that would be useful in designing or tailoring additional procedures to perform to respond to the identified risks. Such procedures might include other risk assessment procedures and further audit procedures (that is, tests of controls, when appropriate, and substantive procedures). This process would be iterative. The groupings and filtering would be refined and reperformed as required to meet the objectives of the ADA.

2.21 As an illustration of this process, consider a case in which an auditor has used an ADA to identify and assess risks of misstatement related to the adequacy of the audited company's allowance for doubtful accounts (that is, the valuation assertion for accounts receivable). The ADA used a model developed by the auditor that included, for example, characteristics of customers likely to affect whether they would pay amounts owed when due. These characteristics included, for example, the amount owed, whether the customer is long-standing or a new customer, the payment history of the customer, the location of the customer, and the currency in which the receivable was denominated (that is, in relation to risks associated with fluctuations in foreign exchange rates).

2.22 In this example, the initial performance of the ADA identified a large number of notable items. These were amounts owed from customers whose characteristics indicated that they would be unlikely to pay amounts owed when due. From a review of the output from the ADA, it appeared that a significant number of notable items represented amounts owed from new related parties. These resulted from a number of significant acquisitions made by the company during the year. The auditor had planned other procedures to specifically address assertions pertaining to related party transactions. Identifying this type of account receivable was not an intended objective of the ADA. As indicated in the second box in exhibit 2-2, the auditor redesigned the model used for the ADA to exclude related parties. The ADA was then reperformed, resulting in a significant reduction of the number of notable items identified. The refined ADA provided information that enabled the auditor to perform appropriately tailored additional procedures on the notable items, and the other items remaining in the population, based on their characteristics.

2.23 In another scenario using this same example, the initial application of the ADA identified a large number of notable items. The auditor decided to use the ADA to identify, as a separate group, notable items representing accounts receivable from large companies in specified industries and located in a G7 country (that is, Canada, France, Germany, Italy, Japan, the United Kingdom or the United States). The auditor decided on this grouping because, based on other risk assessment procedures performed, the auditor concluded that the amounts receivable from customers in this group would not likely present new or higher risks of collectability. After performing the sorting procedure (step *b* in paragraph 2.19), these items were placed in category *bi* (that is, items requiring no further response to identify new or higher risks). These items were addressed by further audit procedures designed to respond to items of lower assessed risks of material misstatement.

2.24 The auditor also identified a large number of notable items that required a further response (category *b*ii in paragraph 2.19). Under step *c*, the auditor further analyzed the characteristics in this group. This further analysis identified a group composed of customers whose balances presented higher risks of material misstatement because they operated in particular industries that were located in countries whose currencies had become less stable and were experiencing volatile political and economic environments. The amounts receivable from these customers fell into category *c*ii (that is, items having a higher risk). Other accounts receivable were in group *c*iii because the results of the ADA did not indicate new or higher levels of assessed risk of material misstatement.

2.25 After the grouping and filtering process is complete (in some cases, after one or more refinements), the auditor would design and perform procedures that appropriately respond to the various risks identified for the items in each group (*c*i, *c*ii, and *c*iii). The auditor would also document the procedures performed to filter and sort the notable items, including the common characteristics identified, and document the procedures to be performed to address the risks associated with each group.

Addressing Risks of Material Misstatement for Remaining Population Items

2.26 If there are any risks of material misstatement related to items in the population that have not been identified as notable items (that is, the remaining population items), the auditor performs further audit procedures to respond to those assessed risks. In some cases, the auditor may conclude that a reasonable possibility of material misstatement in the remaining population does not exist.

Using ADAs in Performing Procedures to Assist When Forming an Overall Conclusion

2.27 Paragraph .06 of AU-C section 520, *Analytical Procedures*, states that the auditor should design and perform analytical procedures near the end of the audit that assist the auditor when forming an overall conclusion about whether the financial statements are consistent with the auditor's understanding of the entity. This chapter discusses the use of ADAs in meeting this requirement.

2.28 Paragraph .A27 of AU-C section 520 states that the analytical procedures performed in accordance with paragraph .06 of that section may be similar to those that would be used as risk assessment procedures. However, the auditor's perspective in applying an ADA near the end of the audit is different than when the auditor is using an ADA to assess risks. As the end of the audit approaches, the auditor has performed and reached conclusions based on the audit procedures for the current year. As a result, the auditor has obtained a more up-to-date and perhaps broader and deeper understanding of the entity and the environment in which it operates than the auditor had at the start of the audit. Therefore, the auditor's focus is on whether something significant has been missed that, if identified near the end of the audit, could lead the auditor to revise previous risk assessments and perform further audit procedures in response to changes in assessed risks. Other matters, not necessarily giving rise to changes in risk assessment, might also have come to the auditor's attention that required investigation and resolution.

2.29 For example, the auditor might consider updating ratios and related analyses used in assessing risks of material misstatement. This might be useful, for example, if management has made significant adjustments to the financial statements during the course of the audit. The objective of this procedure would be to assess whether the ratios based on the next-to-final draft of the financial statements seem reasonable in relation to the auditor's understanding of the entity updated as a result of the current year's audit. The auditor might also consider updating year-over-year financial statement analyses for the same reason.

Appendix A

Examples of ADAs Used in Performing Risk Assessment Procedures

Notes:

1. *The examples in this appendix illustrate matters discussed in chapter 2.*

2. *The examples that follow do not address the auditor's approach to considering the reliability of data used in each example. For further information regarding procedures to address reliability of data, refer to paragraphs 1.38–1.44 and appendix D to this guide.*

3. *In the following examples, if a step or a procedure noted in exhibit 2-1 (included in chapter 2) does not present an issue in the context of the particular example, no reference is made to that step or procedure. Also, in some examples, procedures are combined.*

Example 2-1—Non-Statistical Trend Analysis of Sales Revenue [1]

Background Information

A.01 In this example, the financial statements being audited are those of a small manufacturer of nine types of commercial printers. Annual sales are approximately $25 million. This is the fourth year of the auditor's appointment.

Plan the ADA

Determine the Specific Objectives of the ADA Within the Context of Its Overall Purpose

A.02 The objective of this ADA was to help the auditor determine if there were any unusual changes in sales from prior years or other trends in revenue from sales of commercial printers that might affect risks of material misstatement. The auditor considered identified changes and trends in determining the auditor's nature, timing, and extent of audit procedures.

A.03 This ADA was intended to provide information relevant to assessing and responding to risks of material misstatement related to the occurrence, completeness, and accuracy of revenue. In addition, the auditor considered that significant declines in volumes of sales of particular types of printers could be indicative of potential issues regarding inventory valuation (that is, the adequacy of the allowance for obsolete stock) or the completeness of warranty provisions if the decline in sales related to product quality problems.

A.04 The auditor was already aware, for example, of a labor strike that had occurred at the company's Michigan plant for a considerable part of the

---

[1] Some auditors referred to this procedure as a *reasonableness test*.

year. Inquiries confirmed that sales were down significantly due to the strike and had only started to recover in the last quarter of the year. Also, regarding the product sales mix, the auditor was informed that, as anticipated, a new advanced printer (type H) came into production early in the year and quickly became the company's biggest seller. Based on this information, the auditor anticipated sales declines in other printer types. These reduced sales increased a potential risk of obsolescence and overvaluation of inventories of these printer types. The auditor also considered the risk of possible understatements of the warranty provision for the new printer type H, given the lack of experience in claims from customers regarding this printer.

Determine the Data Population to Be Analyzed

A.05 The data used for this ADA consisted of amounts recorded in accounts in the company's general ledger in the current year and the immediately three preceding years regarding sales of the company's printer types. For the current year, quarterly sales data was accessed. The units sold for each printer type were obtained from the company's database. The data was accessed using audit software.

Select the Techniques, Tools and Graphics, and Tables to Be Used

A.06 The auditor decided that the following would be useful:

- A graphic showing quarterly sales over each of the past four years to help reveal any unexpected trends in sales revenue
- A graphic showing trends in sales of each type of printer

Exhibit A-1

Sales Revenue by Quarter—2012–2015

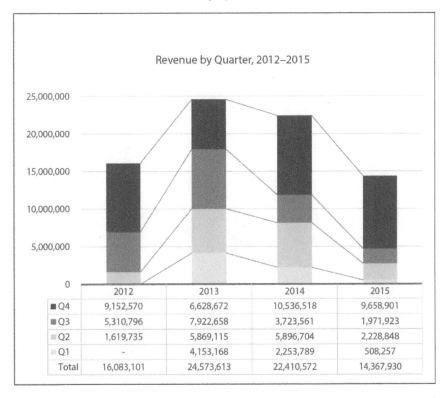

Revenue by Quarter, 2012–2015

	2012	2013	2014	2015
Q4	9,152,570	6,628,672	10,536,518	9,658,901
Q3	5,310,796	7,922,658	3,723,561	1,971,923
Q2	1,619,735	5,869,115	5,896,704	2,228,848
Q1	-	4,153,168	2,253,789	508,257
Total	16,083,101	24,573,613	22,410,572	14,367,930

Exhibit A-2

Number of Printers Sold by Printer Type

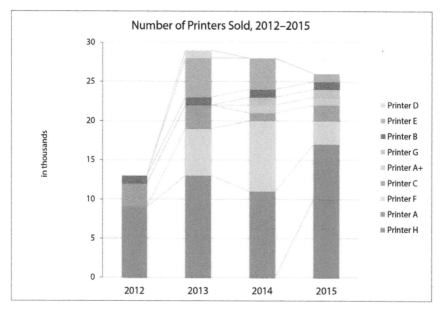

Exhibit A-3

Number of Printers Sold by Year—Alternative Graphic

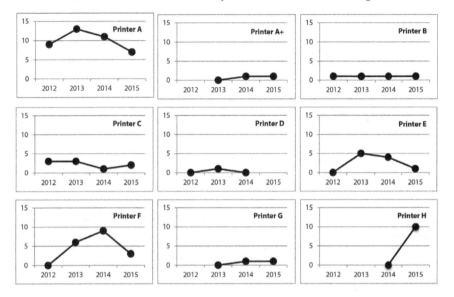

Perform the ADA

A.07 Exhibit A-1 shows the graphic of sales revenue by quarter for each of the current years and the previous three years. The company started operations in Q2 of 2012. As expected, as a result of an extended labor strike, sales revenue for each quarter of the current year is less than the previous years. It is not until the final quarter that sales began to approach last year's levels.

A.08 Exhibit A-2, and the alternate graphic in exhibit A-3, show the unit sales by printer type. The information in the graphic was consistent with information obtained by the auditor by preliminary inquiries of management. For example, there were no sales of printer D in the current year (production was discontinued in 2013). As anticipated, during 2015, new advanced printer H became the biggest seller. Sales of printer F had grown in 2013 and 2014 because at the time, it featured technological advances that strongly appealed to customers. However, the advances made with printer H resulted in printer F losing much of its initial attraction.

Evaluate the Results and Determine Whether the Purpose and Specific Objectives of Performing the ADA Have Been Achieved

A.09 The application of this ADA confirmed the directional changes that the auditor anticipated regarding sales product mix and trends compared to previous years, taking into account information obtained from other sources, including inquiries of management. The results also confirmed the auditor's original risk assessments related to the occurrence, completeness, and accuracy of revenue. The significant declines in volumes of sales of particular types of printers confirmed that there was likely a higher risk of overvaluations of inventory of older printers, and the auditor planned procedures to respond to this higher risk. The results of the ADA did not identify a need to modify planned procedures regarding warranty provisions.

A.10 The auditor determined that the objectives as set out in paragraphs A.02–A.03 had been achieved.

Example 2-2—Preliminary General Ledger Account Balance Analysis

Background Information

A.11 The financial statements being audited are those of a large-sized private company. The auditor is performing an analysis of preliminary year-end balances in the company's general ledger.

Plan the ADA

Determine the Specific Objectives of the ADA Within the Context of Its Overall Purpose

A.12 This ADA was used to assess risks of material misstatement in the company's preliminary general ledger account balances. The auditor's specific objectives in using this ADA were as follows:

- Analyze the preliminary balances in all the accounts in the company's general ledger to identify unusual changes from previous years, including unexpected trends
- Use the results of the analysis to decide whether changes were needed in the planned nature, timing, and extent of the following:
    — Other risk assessment procedures, focused on particular accounts and related assertions
    — Further audit procedures to be performed in response to assessed risks, including tests of controls and substantive procedures

A.13 In deciding what would be considered an unusual change, the auditor considered information obtained from auditing the company's financial statements in each of the previous five years. The auditor also made preliminary inquiries of management regarding significant changes in the current year likely to affect, for example, the relevance of some of the information obtained in previous years. In addition, the auditor made preliminary decisions regarding materiality and performance materiality.

A.14 Based on the auditor's initial work outlined previously, and using professional judgment, the auditor decided on the levels of change in an account balance that would warrant performing more detailed risk assessment procedures. The changes were determined on a year-over-year basis (in this example, 2013 compared to 2012). A matter warranted further consideration by the auditor if the difference between current and prior year (increase or decrease) was $3 million or more. Generally, the auditor should also consider investigating the absence of expected changes in amounts or for instances in which an amount or ratio was expected to increase or decrease, and the opposite occurred.

A.15 The auditor also decided that it would be useful to calculate a number of ratios relevant to the company's operations and financial position to help identify areas of potentially higher risk of material misstatement. The auditor considered whether each ratio for 2013 was likely to significantly increase or decrease from those calculated based on recorded amounts in each of years 2009–2012. The auditor also considered the auditor's understanding of the entity's business obtained in previous years' audits and the results of preliminary inquiries regarding changes in the current year. The ratios used in the ADA included the following:

Liquidity Ratios *Cash Ratio:*	(Cash + Cash Equivalents)/Current Liabilities
Current Ratio or Working Capital Ratio:	Current Assets/Current Liabilities
Quick Ratio:	(Cash and Cash Equivalents + Marketable Securities + Accounts Receivable)/Current Liabilities
Days Sales in Receivables:	Net Accounts Receivable/(Sales Revenue/360)
Leverage Ratios *Total Debt / Equity* *Total Debt / Total Assets* *Long-Term Debt / Equity* *Long-Term Debt / Total Assets*	
Margin Ratios *EBIT Ratio:*	Earnings Before Interest and Taxes/Sales Revenue
EBITDA Ratio:	Earnings Before Interest, Taxes, Depreciation, and Amortization/Sales Revenue
Gross Margin Ratio:	(Sales Revenue—Cost of Sales)/Sales Revenue
Operating Expense Ratio:	Operating Expenses/Sales Revenue
Pre-Tax Margin:	Income Before Taxes/Sales Revenue
Post-Tax Margin:	Net Income/Sales Revenue

Determine the Data Population to Be Analyzed, the Appropriate ADA, Tools, and Visualization Techniques

A.16 The auditor decided to use audit software to access the data in the company's general ledger as of the fiscal year end for 2013 and for the years 2009–2012. The tool calculated the year-over-year changes in amounts and percentage changes in accounts between 2013 and 2012, as well as a trend analysis for the years 2009–2013. It also calculated ratios specified by the auditor as of the fiscal year ends and for the years 2009–2013.

A.17 Using audit software to access appropriate files, tables, and fields in the general ledger, the auditor was able to readily obtain more detail (for example, transaction history) regarding an account balance when the auditor determined that it was warranted.

A.18 Audit software was used to generate graphics to identify matters that indicated areas of possibly higher risk of material misstatement. The graphics used are shown in exhibits A-4, A-5, and A-6.

Perform the ADA

A.19 Exhibit A-4 shows a graphic the auditor developed using the audit software, tailored, as appropriate, to the circumstances of the engagement. Key features of this graphic include the following:

- The increase or decrease in each general ledger account between the end of the current year and the end of the prior year is indicated by a colored bar. For comparative purposes, the change between each balance as of the end of the prior year and the year that preceded it is indicated by a bar outlined in black.

- The auditor's decision on the threshold used to trigger performing more detailed risk assessment procedures (see paragraph A.14) is incorporated into the graphic. A change of $3 million or more is represented by a yellow bar that indicated that the change required further consideration. A change of less than $3 million is represented by a green bar. The auditor used professional judgment and skepticism in determining whether other relationships warranted additional consideration and in determining the nature and extent of the more detailed risk assessment procedures performed.

- The word "pass" in the exhibit means that there was no indication that more detailed risk assessment procedures were warranted. However, as required by paragraph .18 of AU-C section 330, *Performing Audit Procedures in Response to Assessed Risks and Evaluating the Audit Evidence Obtained*, irrespective of the assessed risks of material misstatement, the auditor should design and perform substantive procedures for all relevant assertions related to each material class of transactions, account balance, and disclosure.

Exhibit A-4

Changes in General Ledger Account Balances

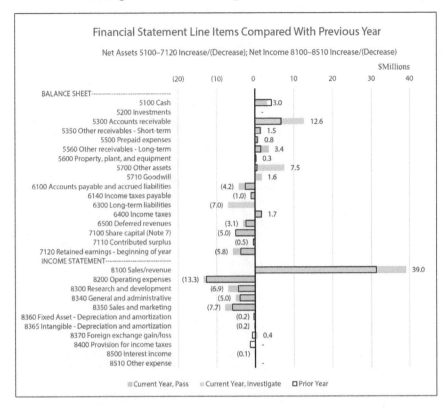

Financial Statement Line Items Compared With Previous Year

Net Assets 5100–7120 Increase/(Decrease); Net Income 8100–8510 Increase/(Decrease)

$Millions

BALANCE SHEET	
5100 Cash	3.0
5200 Investments	-
5300 Accounts receivable	12.6
5350 Other receivables - Short-term	1.5
5500 Prepaid expenses	0.8
5560 Other receivables - Long-term	3.4
5600 Property, plant, and equipment	0.3
5700 Other assets	7.5
5710 Goodwill	1.6
6100 Accounts payable and accrued liabilities	(4.2)
6140 Income taxes payable	(1.0)
6300 Long-term liabilities	(7.0)
6400 Income taxes	1.7
6500 Deferred revenues	(3.1)
7100 Share capital (Note 7)	(5.0)
7110 Contributed surplus	(0.5)
7120 Retained earnings - beginning of year	(5.8)
INCOME STATEMENT	
8100 Sales/revenue	39.0
8200 Operating expenses	(13.3)
8300 Research and development	(6.9)
8340 General and administrative	(5.0)
8350 Sales and marketing	(7.7)
8360 Fixed Asset - Depreciation and amortization	(0.2)
8365 Intangible - Depreciation and amortization	(0.2)
8370 Foreign exchange gain/loss	0.4
8400 Provision for income taxes	-
8500 Interest income	(0.1)
8510 Other expense	-

■ Current Year, Pass ■ Current Year, Investigate □ Prior Year

Exhibit A-5

Analysis Showing Accounts Receivable (Net of Allowance for Doubtful Accounts) by Year and Currency

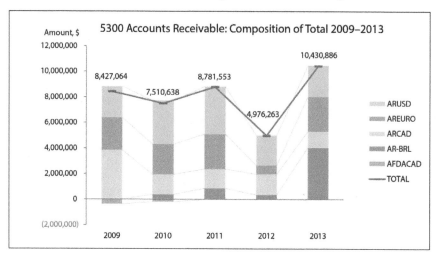

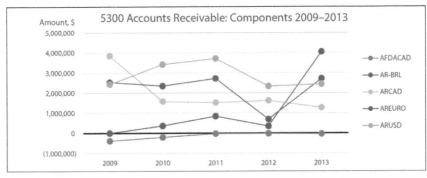

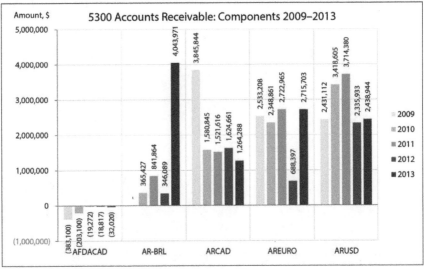

A.20 Exhibit A-5 shows in graphic form the more detailed information obtained regarding general ledger account 5300, Accounts Receivable.

Exhibit A-6

Ratios Used in This Example in Assessing Risks of Material Misstatement

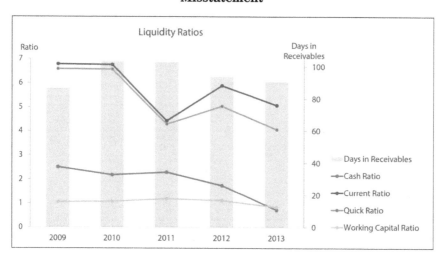

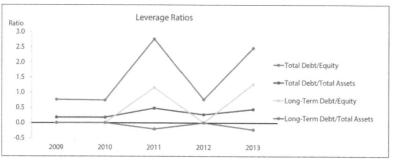

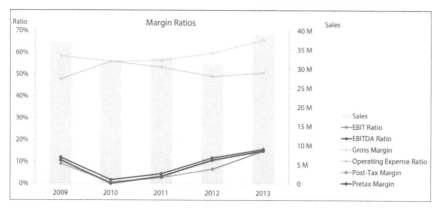

A.21 Exhibit A-6 shows a graphic of five-year trends on various ratios. The auditor used this graphic in considering whether the amounts and directions of changes in ratios over recent years, including ratios for the current year based on recorded amounts, appeared to indicate higher risks of material misstatement in relevant accounts.

Evaluate the Results and Determine Whether the Purpose and Specific Objectives of Performing the ADA Have Been Achieved

A.22 The auditor considered the significant changes shown in exhibit A-4 (those in yellow) to be notable items. For example, there was a significant change in accounts receivable, both in amount and percentage, between 2013 and 2012. In previous years, accounts receivable from entities in foreign countries presented risks of material misstatement regarding appropriate accounting for foreign exchange. Similar to what the auditor encountered in the audits of previous years, political and economic instability in various countries where customers were located were a significant factor in risks affecting collectability of accounts (that is, the valuation assertion). Therefore, as part of the further consideration of this change and to consider in more detail the changes related to the accounts receivable from foreign entities, the auditor used the audit software to add in the currencies in which amounts were receivable in years 2009–2013.

A.23 Using information in exhibit A-5, the auditor considered the effect on risks of material misstatement related to valuation of accounts receivable as a result of significant increases in the amounts of accounts receivable from customers in Britain and other countries in Europe. The auditor discussed with management the reasons for the changes in the balances to obtain a more thorough understanding of the activity during the year to help inform the auditor's risk assessments and to assist in planning appropriate procedures to respond to the risks.

A.24 The auditor determined that the objectives, as set out in paragraph A.12, had been achieved.

Example 2-3—Analysis of Customer Accounts Receivable Churn

Background Information

A.25 The financial statements being audited in this example are those of a large, long-established manufacturing company. The auditor has been auditing the company for five years. This example focuses on the approach taken by the auditor to assess risks of material misstatement related to the customer balances that make up the company's accounts receivable. The auditor used an ADA that provided the auditor with a detailed analysis of changes in the composition of the open accounts receivable balance by customer. These changes are sometimes encompassed in the term *accounts receivable churn*.

A.26 Accounts receivable churn may be affected by various types of products or services and various levels of maturity in the marketplace. Some examples follow:

- A seasoned manufacturer of industrial cleaning supply products might experience very low customer churn because it has achieved a high level of market penetration. Its established base of customers may continually buy its products.

- A manufacturer of enterprise routers, switches, and other networking equipment might have a cyclical customer churn based on the useful life of the equipment it sells. Its customers might not need to purchase new equipment every year. New customers might appear in year one, make large purchases, and return again only three years later when the equipment has to be replaced.
- A new business focused on growth and market expansion, in its first several years of operation, might experience a high increase in accounts receivable from a widening mix of new customers. That growth and changing mix in its customer base might stabilize as the business matures.

Plan the ADA

Determine the Specific Objectives of the ADA Within the Context of Its Overall Purpose

A.27 This ADA was performed primarily to assist in identifying and assessing risks related to the accounts receivable valuation assertion. That is, it was used to assist in identifying possible risks regarding the collectability of accounts receivable and, therefore, the adequacy of the company's allowance for doubtful accounts.

A.28 The company being audited had a stable base of customers for many years. Nothing came to the auditor's attention in performing preliminary planning procedures to indicate that previous trends in the number of customers, and average amounts receivable from them, should change significantly in the current year. The level of "churn" expected by the auditor was based on past experience in auditing the entity in previous years and an updated understanding of the entity resulting from inquiries of management, corroborated by other procedures.

A.29 In using this ADA, the auditor categorized customers into three main groups:

- *Common.* Customers who had a balance outstanding as of the current period end date and the corresponding period end date in the previous year.
- *New.* Customers who had a balance outstanding as of the current period end date but did not have a balance outstanding as of the corresponding period end date in the previous year.
- *Fully cleared.* Customers who had a balance outstanding as of the period end date in the previous year but had no balance outstanding as of the current year period end date.

A.30 The auditor used this categorization to help assess risks of material misstatement. For example, based on prior experience, the auditor considered there was likely a higher risk related to collectability of accounts receivable from new customers who had no payment history with the entity. If the ADA indicated that there were few new customers, the auditor might assess the risk of material misstatement as being lower than a circumstance in which there were many new customers.

Exhibit A-7

Examples of Files, Tables, and Fields From Which Data Was Accessed Using This ADA

	Customer_ Master_ YYYY MMDD file	Open_ Accounts_ Receivable_ YYYYMMDD table	Invoices_ Generated_ YYYYMMDD_ YYYYMMDD file	AR_Cash_ Application_ YYYYMMDD_ YYYYMMDD file
Relevant Fields				
Customer_Account_ID	X	X	X	X
Customer_Account_Name	X			
Customer_Physical_Street_ Address City	X			
Customer_Physical_State_ Province	X			
Customer_Physical_Zip PostalCode	X			
Customer_Physical_Country	X			
Active_Date	X			
Inactive_Date	X			
Entered_Date	X		X	X
Transaction_ID		X		
Transaction_Date		X		
Transaction_Type		X		
Transaction_Due_Date		X		
Balance_Amount		X		
Original_Balance_Amount		X		
AR_Application_ID				X
AR_Application_Date				X
AR_Application_Fiscal_Year				X
AR_Application_Period				X
Receipt_ID				X
Invoice_ID			X	X
AR_Application_Amount				X
GL_Line_Debit_Account_ Number				X
GL_Line_Credit_Account_ Number				X
Invoice_Number			X	
Invoice_Fiscal_Year			X	
Invoice_Date			X	
Invoice_Period			X	
Invoice_Due_Date			X	
Invoice_Amount			X	
Sales_Order_ID			X	

Determine the Data Population to Be Analyzed, the Appropriate ADA, Tools, and Visualization Techniques

A.31 Exhibit A-7 shows the types of data used for this ADA, extracted from fields within tables and files in the company's database. These examples are taken from the AICPA Order to Cash Audit Data Standard.[2] Not all this data was used in the initial analysis of changes in accounts receivable from the previous year. Some were used in subsequent, more in-depth analyses to obtain additional information when warranted.

A.32 The AICPA Audit Data Standards referred to in paragraph A.31 have checklists that are useful in determining whether data is appropriate for use. When reviewing the underlying details of the analysis, the auditor considered whether the data fields were consistently populated. For example, the audit software was used to check that the credit limit field had been completed for all new customers. If the field was empty, the auditor considered that that could be an indication that no credit limit was set for the customer, or that the company tracked each customer's credit limit outside its enterprise resource planning (ERP) system (that is, within a separate customer relationship management system). Overall, the auditor considered the effect of the frequency and nature of occurrences of inaccurate or missing data on the auditor's assessment of risks of material misstatement (including controls risk) for accounts receivable being assessed by using this ADA.

A.33 The auditor decided that the graphics and tables shown in exhibits A-8, A-9, and A-10 would be useful in drawing attention to key changes in accounts receivable from the previous year.

---

[2] See   www.aicpa.org/interestareas/frc/assuranceadvisoryservices/downloadabledocuments/ auditdatastandards/auditdatastandards.gl.july2015.pdf.

Exhibit A-8

Example Table Showing Initial Results of Accounts Receivable Churning ADA

Customers	A 12/31/2015		B 12/31/2014		C Change Between Years	
	No.	$	No.	$	No.	$
New[a]	450	7,534,232	0	—	450	7,534,232
Common[b]	2380	79,342,343	2380	89,432,112	0	(10,089,769)
Fully cleared[c]	0	—	540	4,432,553	(540)	(4,432,553)
Total	2830	86,876,575	2920	93,864,665	(90)	(6,988,090)

Notes:

[a] Customer accounts that have outstanding balances in the current period only.

[b] Customer accounts that have outstanding balances in both the current and prior periods.

[c] Customer accounts that have outstanding balances in the prior period only.

Exhibit A-9

Example Graphic Showing Initial Results of Accounts Receivable Churning ADA

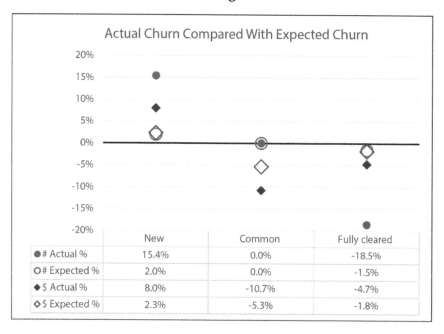

	New	Common	Fully cleared
● # Actual %	15.4%	0.0%	-18.5%
○ # Expected %	2.0%	0.0%	-1.5%
◆ $ Actual %	8.0%	-10.7%	-4.7%
◇ $ Expected %	2.3%	-5.3%	-1.8%

Perform the ADA

A.34 Exhibit A-10 shows in table form the initial results of the ADA. Exhibit A-9 shows those same results using a graphic based on percentage changes. As indicated in column 3 of exhibit A-8, during 2015, the company had 540 customer account balances that were no longer outstanding as of the period end (fully cleared) and added 450 new outstanding customer accounts as of the period end, for a net decrease of 90 outstanding customer accounts. The dollar value of these outstanding customer accounts decreased from $93,864,665 at the end of 2014 to $86,876,575 at the end of 2015, a decrease of $6,988,090.

Exhibit A-10

Table Comparing Auditor's Expected Changes in Customer Balances With Results of Accounts Receivable Churning ADA

	A Auditor's Expected Change Between Years		B Change Between Years (column 3 above)		C Difference (B–A)	
Customers	No.	$	No.	$	No.	$
New[a]	—	2,179,438	—	7,534,232	—	5,354,794
Common[b]	—	(10,000,000)	—	(10,089,769)	—	(89,769)
Fully cleared[c]	—	(1,653,366)	—	(4,432,553)	—	(2,779,187)
Total	—	(9,473,928)	—	(6,988,090)	—	(2,514,162)

Notes:

[a] Customer accounts that have outstanding balances in the current period only.

[b] Customer accounts that have outstanding balances in both the current and prior periods.

[c] Customer accounts that have outstanding balances in the prior period only.

Apply the Process for Notable Items

A.35 As indicated in exhibit A-10, there were significant changes in the composition of the accounts receivable. The auditor was concerned that new customers might be linked to a higher risk of uncollectible accounts.

A.36 The auditor followed the process for addressing notable items set out in exhibit 2-2 (noted in chapter 2). Given the results of the previously noted ADA, the auditor considered all new and fully cleared accounts to be notable items. As mentioned previously, new customers are considered to represent a potentially higher risk of collection. Fully cleared balances could simply represent a timing difference, or they could represent a loss of customers due to product or other issues, thereby warranting further auditor consideration. The auditor decided that redesigning and reperforming the ADA was not warranted because the difference in the results compared with the auditor's expectations was not a result of the ADA used. Using audit software, the auditor accessed and analyzed data at a more disaggregated level to determine whether any notable items had common characteristics. This included accessing the address fields in the database for all new and lost customers to see whether the customers had a location in common. The auditor also accessed the product type fields of goods purchased by the new and lost customers to see if there were any commonalities in these product types.

A.37 Further analysis revealed that the fully cleared accounts were from various locations and were simply the result of timing differences. These amounts were included in the scope of the auditor's substantive audit procedures. Also, it was shown that most of the new accounts receivable were from companies located in various countries in Western Europe.

A.38 The auditor performed procedures to determine whether the results of the analysis indicated a need for a change in the assessed risks of material misstatement. These procedures included further inquiries of management regarding what had occurred that would give rise to these results, corroborated by reference to relevant documentation. Regarding the new customers located in Western Europe, management indicated that they were the result of additional marketing efforts targeted at European companies, a market that had not previously been actively pursued. Technological advances and the bankruptcy of a major competitor enabled the company to successfully make some inroads into this market for the first time.

Evaluate the Results and Determine Whether the Purpose and Specific Objectives of Performing the ADA Have Been Achieved

A.39 The auditor decided to plan more extensive procedures regarding the collectibility of accounts receivable from the new customers located in Western Europe. These were to include specific tests of aging on these accounts, the comparison of invoiced amounts and outstanding balances against credit limits, and reperforming the company's credit checks using external credit ratings for the largest new customers and a sample of smaller customers. The auditor also decided to send confirmation requests to those same new customers to provide added assurance that these new accounts were not fictitious. Further, the auditor considered that the risk of fictitious customers being included in the accounts could be other than low, given the large number of customers lost by the company during the year and the strong incentive for management to present a more stable financial picture than what might, in fact, be the case.

A.40 The auditor performed a final review of the results of the ADA and the appropriateness of the actions planned, taking into account the results of other procedures relevant to identifying and responding to the risks of material misstatement being addressed by this ADA.

A.41 The auditor determined that the objectives, as set out in paragraph A.25, had been achieved.

Example 2-4—Quantity and Pricing Analysis of Sales Revenue

Background Information

A.42 In this example, the financial statements audited are those of a medium-sized manufacturer of two types of computer monitors: 18 inch and 22 inch. The company sells most of these products to retail stores. The auditor has audited the financial statements of this company for the three previous years.

Plan the ADA

Determine the Specific Objectives of the ADA Within the Context of Its Overall Purpose and the Data Population to Be Analyzed

A.43 This ADA was used to assess the risks of material misstatement related to the accuracy of sales revenue. Material misstatements might result from pricing or quantity errors in preparing invoices, including, for example, the application of customer discount rates that do not comply with the company's policies.

A.44 In addition, there might be instances when, for example, the sale of a high quantity of goods at a price significantly different from the average price might indicate a risk of the existence of a related party that management has not made known to the auditor or different sales terms that could affect revenue recognition.

A.45 The auditor decided that it would be useful to perform an ADA to compare the units sold and amount billed for every sales invoice in the population of those invoices for the year under audit. The auditor's objective was to use the analysis of pricing and quantity data disaggregated to the individual sales invoice level to help identify transactions with a higher risk of material misstatement on which the auditor likely should focus.

A.46 This ADA enabled the auditor to readily identify even small variations from average price charged per unit sold. The standard price is $249.99 for an 18-inch monitor and $399.99 for a 22-inch monitor. However, the auditor expected variations in the average price charged. For example, customers are allowed different discounts, and prices charged for customers in various geographic areas may differ (due to local market conditions).

A.47 The auditor used professional judgment in determining the nature and extent of variations that would warrant performing further risk assessment procedures, or changes to further planned procedures in response to assessed risks.

Exhibit A-11

18-inch Monitor: Net Sale Value per Transaction

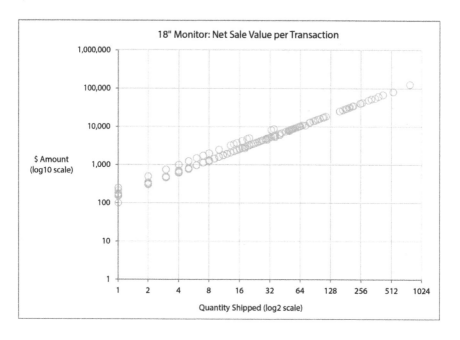

Exhibit A-12

22-inch Monitor: Net Sale Value per Transaction

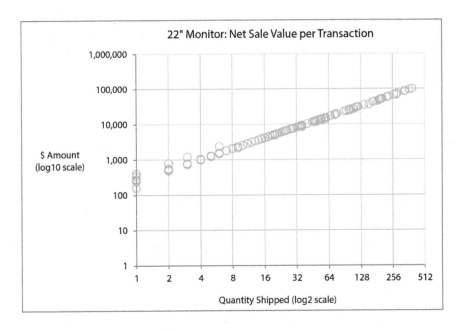

Exhibit A-13

18-inch Monitor: Discount Percent per Transaction

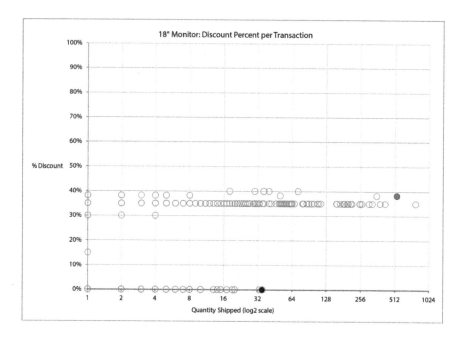

Exhibit A-14

22-inch Monitor: Discount Percent per Transaction

Determine the Data Population to Be Analyzed, the Appropriate ADA, Tools, and Visualization Techniques

A.48 The auditor decided to use an ADA that would plot the relationship between the prices and quantities for each of the company's sales invoices on a graphic. The horizontal axis showed quantity shipped per invoice, and the vertical axis showed the amount billed per invoice. Quantities shipped are shown on a log base 2 scale to be able to more clearly show the effect of what was happening at both the low and high ends of the scale.[3] There were a number of invoices showing zero units shipped. These were not plotted on the graphics because log scales can deal only with positive numbers, however, they were addressed separately. Exhibits A-11 and A-12 show the graphics of the data points resulting from the quantities shipped and amounts billed on each invoice.

A.49 Using this approach, a perfect match among prices and quantities would result in each data point falling on a straight line. Data points that are not on a straight line might represent items with a higher risk of material misstatement because the relationship between quantities and prices is different than expected. The decision about how far off the straight line a data point would need to be to warrant investigation would be a matter of professional judgment for the auditor.

A.50 The auditor expected that discounts offered to customers were likely to have a significant effect on revenues, and that variations in discount rates offered might indicate a higher risk of material misstatement. Because the

---

[3] The numbers used on the horizontal axis of exhibit A-11 range from 20 (that is, 1) to 210 (that is, 1024). In exhibit A-12, the high end of the scale is 29 (that is, 512).

standard price for each type of monitor was known, the auditor decided to use the ADA to compare the standard price with the net price charged on each invoice and produce graphics showing the discount rates offered. The data showed that the standard discount rate appeared to be close to 35 percent. Therefore, the auditor decided that it would be useful to develop graphics showing the extent to which the discount on each invoice varied from 35 percent (exhibits A-13 and A-14). The vertical axis in these graphics represents the difference between a discount of 35 percent and the discount actually given to the customer on each invoice. Paragraph A.52 notes some of the auditor's detailed findings from exhibit A-13 for illustrative purposes.

Access and Prepare the Data for Purposes of the ADA

A.51 The auditor used audit software to apply the ADA. Data accessed from fields within files and tables in the company's database included the following:

- Customer account ID
- Invoice number
- Invoice amount
- Invoice date
- Sales order unit price
- Shipping unit price
- Customer discount percentage
- Sales order quantity
- Sales order ID
- Shipping quantity
- Shipping document ID
- Shipping date
- Shipping product code
- Shipping product description

Perform the ADA

A.52 The preliminary results of the application of the ADA are shown in exhibits A-11, A-12, A-13, and A-14. Many invoices had similar average prices, so many of the dots on the graphic represent multiple invoices. Exhibits A-13 and A-14 clearly show that most invoices have discount rates close to 35 percent (that is, the difference between the expected discount and that actually offered is zero). In addition, the graphics enabled the auditor to focus on those invoices for which the discount was significantly over or under 35 percent because these may indicate a higher risk of material misstatement. For example, the small red circle near the right side of exhibit A-13 represents an invoice for 531, 18-inch monitors for which the discount was $4,313.58 more than expected. In tracking the detail supporting the graphic, the auditor found that the gross amount of the invoice at standard prices would have been $132,744.69. The net amount of the invoice with a 35 percent discount would have been $86,204.05. However, the actual invoice amount was $81,970.47, representing a discount of 38.5 percent. At the other end of the spectrum, the lower half of the middle of exhibit A-13 shows a small black circle representing an invoice for 35 units for which a discount of 35 percent would have amounted to $3,062.38. However, in this case, the auditor found the customer did not receive any discount. The auditors modified their audit plan to address the items identified.

Evaluate the Results and Determine Whether the Purpose and Specific Objectives of Performing the ADA Have Been Achieved

Apply the Process for Notable Items

A.53 In response to the preliminary results, the auditor performed the process for identifying and addressing notable items described in chapter 2, exhibit 2-2. The audit software allowed the auditor to drill down to get the details underlying the dots on each graphic when warranted.

A.54 The dots on exhibits A-11 and A-12 will fall on a straight line if they all have the expected relationship between amounts shipped and amounts invoiced. The items that did not fall on the straight line were considered to be notable items. The auditor concluded that the ADA had been appropriately planned and applied so that there was no need to redesign and reperform it. The auditor performed the filtering process set out exhibit 2-2 in chapter 2 to identify notable items, or groups of notable items, that had similar characteristics. The auditor found that notable items fell into the following groups:

a. 12 invoices for which both the dollar amount and quantity were zero

b. 16 invoices for which the dollar amount billed was zero, but the invoice contained a quantity

c. 23 invoices containing a dollar amount invoiced, but no quantity

d. A few hundred invoices for which the unit price per invoice range departed from the average unit price per invoice

In the process of performing this pricing ADA, the auditor also identified an unusual quantity for an individual invoice (that is, 1 invoice showing the sale of 780, 18-inch monitors to one customer, a highly unusual quantity for an individual invoice). After inquiring with management, the auditor determined that it was a related party not previously identified and planned and performed other procedures as a result.

A.55 The auditor asked management to determine the causes of notable items identified. The auditor obtained and corroborated management's explanations that items 1–3 related to the use of a sub-process to deal with adjustments to particular types of sales transactions. The auditor verified that the adjustments were authorized to eliminate the auditor's initial concerns that these items might be indicative of fraud and, therefore, qualitatively material. The auditor concluded that these notable items did not indicate new or higher risks of material misstatement for relevant assertions and that no further action was required regarding assessment of risks for these notable items.

A.56 Item 4 was an individual notable item. The auditor made inquiries of management about this customer, in particular, whether it was a related party. Management responded that this customer was a subsidiary company formed during the year to explore whether the company should become a retailer as well as a manufacturer and wholesaler. Because this customer was a related party that was not previously identified, the auditor determined that there was a higher risk of a material misstatement related to the existence of undisclosed related parties. The auditor planned and performed procedures that included increased alertness and more proactive searching for possible related parties when performing various audit procedures.

A.57   For notable items in category 5, the auditor performed a filtering process by first accessing the customer name and discount fields for this group of invoices. The auditor found that the vast majority of the items related to three customers with better than average discount rates, although the rates appeared to be within authorized ranges. Consistent with the approach taken in previous years, the auditor intended to rely on the effective operation of controls over discounts offered to customers. Therefore, the auditor amended planned tests of controls to specifically include tests targeted at the discount rates given to these three customers. If the tests identified a deficiency in controls over approval of discounts, the auditor planned to undertake substantive audit procedures in response to the control deficiency identified.

A.58   The auditor determined that the objectives, as set out in paragraphs A.43–A.45, had been achieved.

Example 2-5—Process Mining—Revenue Process From Sales Order to Sales Invoice

Background Information

A.59   The financial statements being audited in this example are those of a medium-sized pet food production company that uses an ERP system. The auditor has audited this company's financial statements for the past three years.

A.60   The auditor used a process-mining ADA to help obtain an understanding of the business process, the related transaction flows through the system, and the entity's internal control. The focus was on the company's financial accounting process for revenues, from sales order to cash receipt. Using this ADA, the auditor was able to analyze, for example, where and how employees might circumvent controls, or take advantage of gaps in controls that had not previously been identified, to perform unauthorized actions. Such actions could increase the risk of material misstatement due to error or fraud.

Exhibit A-15

Example Event Log (Audit Log)

Process instance	Event Description	Timestamp	Originator
534000000821	Create PO	01 Jan 2016	Jane
534000000821	Change line	01 Jan 2016	Jane
534000000821	Authorization	04 Jan 2016	Adam
534000000821	Release	08 Jan 2016	Peter
534000000821	Process	08 Jan 2016	Melinda
534000000821	Prepare shipment	09 Jan 2016	Karl
534000000821	Ship goods	10 Jan 2016	Doug
534000000821	Payment	15 Jan 2016	Brian

A.61 Often, in more complex accounting software packages, actions taken within the system, including the transfer of information into or out of the system, leave a digital trace. Ordinarily, that trace is in the form of system event logs. These are also known as *transaction logs* or *audit trail*. Exhibit A-15 shows an example. Logs are produced automatically by an ERP system. They show, for example, who initiated a task, the nature of the task, and when it was performed. The auditor used a process-mining ADA to access the data in the logs, and from that data, created visualizations of process flows for significant classes of transactions for further analysis.

Plan the ADA

Determine the Specific Objectives of the ADA Within the Context of Its Overall Purpose

A.62 This process-mining ADA focused on obtaining information on the revenue process for use in assessing risks of material misstatement. The relevant assertions included occurrence, completeness, accuracy, and cut-off of sales revenue.

A.63 Possible misstatements of revenue due to fraud were also considered in performing this ADA. Paragraph .26 of AU-C section 240, *Consideration of Fraud in a Financial Statement Audit*, states that when identifying and assessing the risks of material misstatement due to fraud, the auditor should, based on a presumption that risks of fraud exist in revenue recognition, evaluate which types of revenue, revenue transactions, or assertions give rise to such risks.

A.64 This ADA first focused on identifying any variant process path in the company system processing transactions from sales order to sales invoice. A *variant process path* is a path taken in processing transactions that is outside the standard process flow. The auditor has knowledge of the characteristics of that standard process flow based on training and experience in systems of internal control, including information obtained in auditing the company's financial statements in previous years.

A.65 Based on the results of procedures performed in previous years, the auditor expected to identify one or more variant process paths. However, the auditor did not expect any variant process path identified to indicate a higher risk of material misstatement.

A.66 The auditor's focus was on whether a variant process path indicates a higher risk of material misstatement. An example of a variant process path that likely would not indicate a higher risk of material misstatement is a path used to process only a small number of manual sales invoices for legitimate business purposes. A variant process path that might indicate the existence of higher risks of material misstatement would be a path used to process a large volume of sales transactions, with the possibility of the following:

- Goods being shipped without invoices
- Goods authorized for shipment by the same employee who processed the sales order
- Manual override of master pricing data by inappropriate staff
- Irregular timing of processing of certain transactions (for example, near year-end)

Exhibit A-16

Flow Diagram of Sales Order to Sales Invoice Process Created Using a Process-Mining ADA

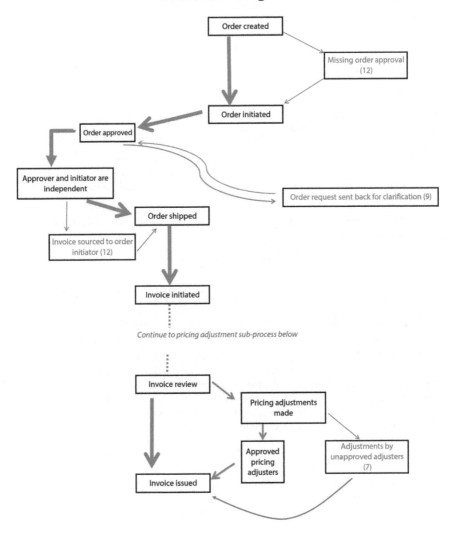

A.67 In general, the auditor determined that any identified variant process path would be investigated. Such investigation might, for example, provide evidence of the following:

- The auditor did not fully understand the process (the auditor would then update his or her understanding).

- A new process was implemented during the year or that existed in previous years but of which the auditor was not aware.

- A potentially new fraud risk or other significant risk.

Select the Techniques, Tools, Graphics, and Tables to Be Used

A.68 Flow diagrams are a core feature of a process-mining ADA. The company's logs were assessed to determine, for example, the volumes and types of activity. A process visualization platform was used to produce the variant flow diagram shown in exhibit A-16. The thicker lines in the flow diagram indicate a higher frequency of transactions through a path. The thinner lines represent process variant paths (that is, flow paths used with less frequency).

Access and Prepare the Data for Purposes of the ADA

A.69 The data was obtained from the company's system event logs.

Evaluate the Results and Conclude Whether the Purpose and Specific Objectives of Performing the ADA Have Been Achieved

A.70 The auditor found that the flow diagram provided a better perspective and more specific information on transactions compared to that obtained in previous years by walking a small number of individual items through the company's system.

A.71 As shown in the flow diagram in exhibit A-16, the auditor identified process flow variants indicating the following:

- 12 instances of missing order approvals
- 9 order requests sent back for clarification
- 12 invoices sourced to the order initiator (that is, the same person initiated the order and the invoice)
- 7 pricing adjustments made by unapproved adjusters

A.72 Through inquiry and other procedures, the auditor obtained an understanding of each of the process flow variants and determined their impact on the auditor's risk assessment and design of further audit procedures. For example, the auditor found overrides of segregation of duties. After further investigation, it was determined that orders were initiated by two employees. Some of these related to transactions that were recorded near year end, resulting in increased risk of misstatements related to cutoff. Therefore, the auditor increased the planned extent of cut-off procedures related to revenues. In response to the manual pricing adjustments made by individuals not authorized to do so, the auditor planned further audit procedures that include the examination of details of pricing adjustments made by those unauthorized individuals.

Chapter 3

Using ADAs in Performing Substantive Analytical Procedures

Matters Covered in This Chapter

3.01 This chapter discusses the concepts and definitions found in AU-C section 520, *Analytical Procedures*. It also discusses matters related to the use of ADAs in performing substantive analytical procedures. The auditor designs and performs these procedures to meet the requirements in AU-C section 520 and other relevant requirements in generally accepted auditing standards (GAAS). Additional guidance on analytical procedures can be found in AICPA Audit Guide *Analytical Procedures*.

3.02 Appendix B sets out the following examples of the use of ADAs in performing substantive analytical procedures.

- Example 3-1—Non-Statistical Predictive Model for Rental Revenue

- Example 3-2—Regression Analysis of Revenue From Sales of Steam

Definition of Analytical Procedures

3.03 Paragraph .04 of AU-C section 520 defines *analytical procedures* as follows:

> **Analytical procedures.** Evaluations of financial information through analysis of plausible relationships among both financial and nonfinancial data. Analytical procedures also encompass such investigation, as is necessary, of identified fluctuations or relationships that are inconsistent with other relevant information or that differ from expected values by a significant amount.

Nature and Objectives of Substantive Analytical Procedures

3.04 Paragraph .04 of AU-C section 330, *Performing Audit Procedures in Response to Assessed Risks and Evaluating the Audit Evidence Obtained*, defines a *substantive procedure* as an audit procedure designed to detect material misstatements at the assertion level. That paragraph also states that substantive procedures comprise

    a. tests of details (classes of transactions, account balances, and disclosures) and

    b. substantive analytical procedures.

3.05 Paragraph .05 of AU-C section 520 contains required steps for the auditor to take in performing a substantive analytical procedure. This chapter discusses key aspects of performing those steps. Paragraph .05 states that when designing and performing analytical procedures, either alone or in combination with tests of details, as substantive procedures in accordance with AU-C section 330, the auditor should do the following:

a. Determine the suitability of particular substantive analytical procedures for given assertions, taking into account the assessed risks of material misstatement and tests of details, if any, for these assertions

b. Evaluate the reliability of data from which the auditor's expectation of recorded amounts or ratios is developed, taking into account the source, comparability, and nature and relevance of information available and controls over preparation

c. Develop an expectation of recorded amounts or ratios and evaluate whether the expectation is sufficiently precise (taking into account whether substantive analytical procedures are to be performed alone or in combination with tests of details) to identify a misstatement that, individually or when aggregated with other misstatements, may cause the financial statements to be materially misstated

d. Determine the amount of any difference of recorded amounts from expected values that is acceptable without further investigation as required by paragraph .07 and compare the recorded amounts, or ratios developed from recorded amounts, with the expectations

Steps an Auditor Might Follow in Planning, Performing, and Evaluating a Substantive Analytical Procedure

3.06 Exhibit 3-1 shows steps that an auditor might use in planning, performing, and evaluating the results of a substantive analytical procedure. Procedures that might often be performed as part of each step are also set out. An auditor might perform these procedures in a different order than set out in exhibit 3-1, and some might be performed simultaneously.

Exhibit 3-1

Steps an Auditor Might Follow in Planning, Performing, and Evaluating a Substantive Analytical Procedure

1. **Plan the substantive analytical procedure.**

   a. Determine the financial statement item or account and related assertions for which the substantive analytical procedure is to provide audit evidence and the specific objectives of the substantive analytical procedure.

   b. Identify the assessed risks of material misstatement to which the substantive analytical procedure is intended to respond (desired level of assurance).

   c. Identify the nature of the auditor's expectation, including

      i. the independent variables (predictors) to be used;

      ii. sources of the data for those variables; and

      iii. levels of disaggregation of the data.

   d. Determine the desired precision of the auditor's expectation.

   e. Determine the amount of difference from the auditor's expectation that can be accepted without further investigation.

   f. Determine the substantive analytical procedure (for example, trend analysis, ratio analysis, non-statistical predictive modelling, regression analysis) that is most likely to meet the auditor's objectives.

   g. Develop the model to be used, when applicable.

   h. Determine the graphics or tables, if any, that are to be used in applying the procedure.

2. **Obtain the data from which the auditor's expectation of recorded amounts or ratios is to be developed.**

3. **Evaluate the reliability of the data.**

   Take into account the source, comparability, and nature and relevance of information available and controls over preparation of the data.

4. **Apply the substantive analytical procedure.**

   a. Develop the auditor's expectation of the recorded amount or ratio.

   b. Evaluate whether the auditor's expectation is sufficiently precise and, if not, the actions to take to increase the precision.

   c. Perform the substantive analytical procedure and compare the auditor's expectation to the recorded amount or ratio.

(continued)

5. **Evaluate and respond to the results of the substantive analytical procedure.**

    a. Determine whether the difference between the auditor's expectation and the recorded amount is significant.

    b. Investigate any significant difference, identifying possible and probable causes.

    c. Determine whether the substantive analytical procedure has identified a misstatement and evaluate any misstatement.

    d. Conclude on whether the objectives of the substantive analytical procedure have been achieved. If the objectives have not been achieved, plan and perform different procedures to achieve those objectives.

Documentation: The auditor should comply with the relevant documentation requirements in GAAS, including those set out in paragraph .08 of AU-C section 520, *Analytical Procedures*.

3.07 Paragraphs 3.08–3.63 discuss key concepts that affect the auditor's performance of one or more of the steps noted in exhibit 3-1. Evaluating data reliability is discussed in chapter 1 and appendix D to this guide.

Auditor's Expectations

3.08 Expectations are the auditor's predictions of recorded accounts or ratios. In performing analytical procedures, the auditor should develop the expectation in such a way that a significant difference between it and the recorded amount is indicative of a misstatement, unless the auditor can obtain and corroborate explanations for the difference (for example, an unusual event occurred). Expectations are developed by identifying plausible relationships (for example, store square footage and retail sales) that are reasonably expected to exist based on the auditor's understanding of the client and the industry in which the client operates. The auditor may select from a variety of data sources to form expectations. For example, the auditor may use prior-period information (adjusted for expected changes), management's budgets or forecasts, industry data, or nonfinancial data. The source of information determines, in part, the precision with which the auditor predicts an account balance and, therefore, is important to consider in developing an expectation to achieve the desired level of assurance from the analytical procedure.

Precision

3.09 Precision is a measure of the closeness of the auditor's expectation to the correct amount. The desired precision of the expectation varies according to the stage of the audit or the purpose of the analytical procedure. For example, precision is more important for analytical procedures used as substantive tests than for those used in planning. The effectiveness of analytical procedures depends on their precision and purpose. Factors that affect the precision of analytical procedures include

- the type of expectation developed,

- the reliability and other characteristics of the data used in forming the expectation (both internally and externally prepared data), and
- the nature of the account or the assertion.

3.10 For example, an auditor plans to test interest income. Because the nature of the account is relatively objective (interest income can easily be predicted), analytical procedures could be designed to serve as an effective substantive test. If the auditor needs a high level of assurance from a procedure, it is necessary to develop a relatively precise expectation. This is affected by the type of procedure selected (for example, a ratio analysis instead of a simple trend analysis), the level of detail of the data (for example, quarterly versus annual data), and the reliability of the source of the data. In the case of substantive tests, the precision of the expectation is the primary determinant of the level of assurance obtained from the analytical procedure. It affects the ability of the auditor to identify correctly whether a given unexpected difference in an account balance is the result of a misstatement. Because precision is directly related to the level of assurance obtained, it is an important consideration in determining whether the planned level of assurance desired from the analytical procedure is achieved. In addition, the higher the desired level of assurance, the more precise the expectation would need to be.

Level of Assurance

3.11 Level of assurance is the complement of the level of detection risk and the degree to which substantive auditing procedures (including analytical procedures) provide evidence in testing an assertion. The level of assurance is dependent on the restriction of detection risk because inherent and control risk exist independently of an audit of financial statements. Detection risk relates to the auditor's procedures and can be changed at the auditor's discretion. The desired or planned level of assurance is that level needed to achieve an acceptable level of detection risk. It is determined by the acceptable level of audit risk, the risk of material misstatement (in other words, the combined assessment of inherent and control risk), and the planning materiality threshold. The achieved level of assurance is the degree to which the auditing procedure actually reduces audit risk and is a function of the effectiveness of the substantive procedures.

Plausibility and Predictability of Relevant Relationships

3.12 Paragraph .A6 of AU-C section 520 states that a basic premise underlying the application of analytical procedures is that plausible relationships among data may reasonably be expected to exist and continue in the absence of known conditions to the contrary. It is important to consider what makes relationships plausible because various types of data sometimes appear to be related when they are not. This may lead the auditor to erroneous conclusions. In addition, the presence of an unexpected relationship may provide important evidence when appropriately scrutinized.

3.13 The auditor's understanding of the entity and its environment is useful in helping to identify the existence and continuance of plausible relationships. The auditor obtains this understanding in accordance with AU-C section 315, *Understanding the Entity and Its Environment and Assessing the Risks of Material Misstatement*.

3.14 The more predictable the relevant relationships are, the more precise the auditor's expectation will be. The following are factors an auditor may consider in predicting the amount of an account:

- The subjective or objective nature of the items in an account balance (for example, whether the account comprises estimates or the accumulation of transactions)
- Product mix
- Company profile (for example, the number, size, and location of operating units)
- Management's discretion (for example, in making estimates)
- Stability of the environment in which the company operates
- Whether the account is an income statement or balance sheet account

For example, expectations developed for income statement accounts tend to be more precise than expectations for balance sheet accounts because income statement relationships generally are more predictable because they occur over a period of time, rather than at a point in time. Also, expectations formed under stable economic conditions (for example, stable interest rates) or stable environmental factors (for example, no regulatory changes) tend to be more precise than expectations formed in an unstable economy or environment.

3.15 Numerous factors affect the amount of an account balance. Increasing the number of such factors considered in forming an expectation of the account balance may increase the precision of the expectation. Such factors include the following:

- Significant events
- Accounting changes
- Business and industry factors
- Market and economic factors
- Management incentives
- Initial versus a repeat engagement

Level of Disaggregation of Data

3.16 *Data aggregation* refers to the level at which account balances, transactions, accounts, or other groupings are combined for use in a substantive analytical procedure. The following are examples:

- Annual data might be disaggregated to a monthly or weekly level.
- Revenues and cost of sales might be disaggregated by product line.
- Data for operations as a whole might be disaggregated by location.

3.17 A material misstatement is likely to be more easily identified through use of disaggregated data. For example, the risk that material misstatements may be obscured by offsetting factors increases as an entity's operations become more complex and diversified. Disaggregation of the information helps reduce this risk. In addition, the auditor's expectation would likely be more precise when disaggregated data are used. The auditor might also look at data disaggregated in different ways (for example, rental revenue by month and by rental property) as, in some cases, this might increase the likelihood of identifying a material misstatement.

3.18 On the other hand, disaggregation of data may present issues for the auditor to consider. In some cases, an entity's controls that operate effectively for data at a highly-aggregated level may not necessarily operate effectively for disaggregated data. For example, quarterly data may not be subject to the same controls as annual data. Further, interim data will normally not have been audited.

Amount of Acceptable Difference of Recorded Amounts From Expected Values

3.19 Performing substantive analytical procedures includes developing an expectation of what that recorded amount likely should be, absent any material misstatement. Various methods that might be used to develop an auditor's expectation are discussed in paragraphs 3.30–3.62. Paragraph .05 of AU-C section 520 requires the auditor to determine the amount of any difference of recorded amounts from expected values that is acceptable without further investigation. Paragraph .A24 of AU-C section 520 states that the auditor's determination of the amount of difference from the expectation that can be accepted without further investigation is influenced by materiality and the desired level of assurance, while taking into account the possibility that a misstatement, individually or when aggregated with other misstatements, may cause the financial statements to be materially misstated. AU-C section 330 requires the auditor to obtain more persuasive audit evidence the higher the auditor's assessment of risk. Accordingly, as the assessed risk increases, the amount of difference considered acceptable without further investigation decreases in order to achieve the desired level of persuasive evidence.

3.20 The auditor should consider the amount of difference from the expectation that can be accepted without further investigation. This consideration is influenced primarily by performance materiality and the desired level of assurance, taking into account the matters noted in paragraph 3.26 of this guide. Paragraph .11 of AU-C section 320, *Materiality in Planning and Performing an Audit,* requires the auditor to determine performance materiality for purposes of assessing the risks of material misstatement and determining the nature, timing, and extent of further audit procedures.

3.21 In some cases, a substantive analytical procedure may be a ratio analysis. The auditor's expected value of the ratio would be compared to the ratio developed from recorded amounts. A ratio analysis would not normally entail developing an expectation regarding each amount used to calculate the ratio. The auditor uses professional judgment in determining whether the inconsistency between the auditor's expected value for the ratio and the ratio based on recorded amounts is acceptable. In making this determination, the auditor takes into account the matters noted in paragraph 3.20.

3.22 If the difference identified by a substantive analytical procedure is less than the auditor's acceptable threshold, taking into consideration the desired level of assurance from the procedure, the auditor may accept the recorded amounts without further investigation.

Investigation of a Significant Difference

3.23 Paragraph .07 of AU-C section 520 states that if analytical procedures performed in accordance with this section identify fluctuations or relationships that are inconsistent with other relevant information or that differ from expected values by a significant amount, the auditor should investigate such differences as follows:

a. By inquiring of management and obtaining appropriate audit evidence relevant to management's responses

b. By performing other audit procedures as necessary in the circumstances.

3.24 The difference between an auditor's expectation and the recorded book value of an account may be due to any or all of the following three causes:

a. A misstatement

b. Inherent factors that affect the account being audited (for example, the predictability of the account or account subjectivity)

c. Factors related to the reliability of data used to develop the expectation

3.25 The more precise the auditor's expectation is, the more likely the difference between the auditor's expectation and the recorded value will be due to misstatements, as discussed in item *a* in paragraph 3.24. Conversely, the less precise the expectation is, the more likely the difference is due to factors related to the precision of the expectation, as related in items *b* and *c* in paragraph 3.24.

3.26 If the auditor believes that the difference is more likely due to factors related to the precision of the expectation, and a more precise expectation can be developed cost-effectively, the analytical procedure may be reperformed based on the new expectation, and the new difference would be calculated. On the other hand, the auditor may rule out items *b* and *c* in paragraph 3.24 as explanations for the unexpected difference and may then evaluate the unexpected difference as a potential misstatement.

3.27 A key step in the auditor's investigation often might be to obtain from management an explanation of the difference. Normally, additional audit evidence is obtained to either corroborate or contradict management's explanation. The procedures used to obtain this audit evidence may depend, for example, on the nature of the account balance being audited and the nature of the explanation provided by management. Also, when the relevant population is disaggregated, a pattern in the differences may indicate that there is a common explanation for those differences, but that may not necessarily be the case.

3.28 The following are examples of further audit procedures that might be performed:

- Inquiries of persons outside the entity. For example, for a substantive analytical procedure involving costs of purchased goods, the auditor may confirm discounts received with major suppliers.

- Inquiries of persons inside the entity not involved in the financial reporting process. For example, the auditor may ask the entity's marketing director to explain a change in advertising expenditures to determine whether this explanation is similar to that provided by the financial controller. Normally, it would be appropriate to discuss a significant difference with knowledgeable entity personnel in addition to those personnel involved in the financial reporting process.

- Evidence obtained from other auditing procedures. Sometimes, the results of other auditing procedures (particularly those performed on data used to develop an expectation) are sufficient to corroborate or contradict an explanation.

- Examination of supporting evidence. The auditor may examine supporting documentary evidence of transactions. For example, if a difference appears to relate to an increase in cost of sales in one month that is attributed to an unusually large sales contract, the auditor might examine supporting documentation, such as the sales contract and delivery dockets.

3.29 Often, it may not be practicable to identify factors that explain the exact amount of a significant difference. However, the auditor performs the procedures required to obtain sufficient appropriate audit evidence to conclude that the amount of the unexplained portion of the significant difference does not indicate the existence of a material misstatement.

Effectiveness of Method Used to Develop the Auditor's Expectation

3.30 Determining the type of method to be used to develop the auditor's expectation is a matter of professional judgment. One consideration in that determination is whether the method used is likely to provide an expectation that is sufficiently precise, taking into account the auditor's desired level of assurance to be obtained from the substantive analytical procedure. Specific matters the auditor may consider include the following:

- The number and nature of variables used in applying the method
- How the auditor might develop the expectation
- How the auditor might determine what will be considered a significant difference from the auditor's expectation
- How the auditor might respond to any identified significant difference

3.31 Paragraphs 3.32–3.63 provide an overview of the matters noted in paragraph 3.30, in the context of using each of the following four types of procedures as substantive analytical procedures:

- Trend analysis
- Ratio analysis
- Non-statistical predictive modelling[1]
- Regression analysis

Trend Analysis

Number and Nature of Variables

3.32 For the purposes of this guide, a *trend analysis* is a comparison of a financial statement item or an account balance for the current period with the corresponding item or account balance for one or more previous periods.

---

[1] Some auditors refer to this type of testing as *reasonableness testing*.

Developing the Auditor's Expectation

3.33 When using a simple trend analysis, the auditor's expectation may be that there will be no significant change in the revenue or expense account from the preceding year.

3.34 Trend analysis is likely to be more effective when the recorded amount or relationship is fairly predictable (for example, sales in a stable environment). Trend analysis is likely to be less effective when the entity under audit has experienced significant operating or accounting changes. The number of periods used in the trend analysis may be a function of the stability of operations. The more stable the entity's operations are over time, the more predictable the relationships become. It is then more appropriate to use amounts from multiple time periods.

3.35 Trend analysis is less precise when it is based on data aggregated at a high level. For example, trend analysis of an entity's operating units on a consolidated basis is relatively imprecise. A material misstatement is often small relative to the natural variation in an aggregate account balance. Therefore, a trend analysis used as a substantive analytical procedure often would entail the use of disaggregated data. For example, instead of using total sales for the year, the auditor may use sales revenue by segment, product, or location. The auditor may also use monthly or quarterly sales.

3.36 When used as a substantive analytical procedure, trend analysis normally would be one of a number of procedures used to achieve the auditor's objectives regarding the accounts and related assertions being audited. Trend analysis, even when using disaggregated data, is likely to result in a relatively imprecise auditor's expectation that would provide only a low level of assurance.

Determining and Responding to a Significant Difference

3.37 Taking into account performance materiality, the auditor may determine, for example, a percentage change in a financial statement item or recorded amount, or components thereof, that if exceeded would be considered a significant difference from the auditor's expectation.

3.38 If the auditor identifies a significant difference, the auditor would need to perform further procedures to investigate that difference. These procedures might include, for example, a more precise trend analysis or tests to verify the explanations provided by management regarding the differences identified.

Ratio Analysis

Number and Nature of Variables

3.39 For ratio analysis used in a financial statement audit, at least one of the two variables would often be a financial statement item or recorded amount, or a component of the item or amount. For example, the ratio might be a gross profit percentage. The ratio might use total sales and cost of sales for the year, or perhaps sales and cost of sales for each of the entity's operating locations. In some cases, one variable in the ratio may be nonfinancial in nature (for example, number of days in a year or month). A wide range of ratios may be used in obtaining audit evidence.

Developing the Auditor's Expectation

3.40 Ratio analysis will result in a less precise auditor's expectation if it is based on data at a highly-aggregated level. This is because a material misstatement is often small relative to the natural variations in a ratio. This suggests that ratio analysis used as a substantive analytical procedure may need to be based on data at a more disaggregated level (for example, by segment, product, or location).

3.41 Ratio analysis is typically not statistical in nature. However, if desired, it may be practicable for the auditor to introduce some statistical rigor into the ratio analysis.

3.42 Ratio analysis may not involve the use of a model to develop an expectation of the financial statement item or recorded amount in the ratio or of the ratio itself. The ratio for the specified period is compared with the same ratio for one or more previous periods for the same entity or with that for other comparable entities in the current period or both. The change in a ratio from a previous period (or a difference from the ratio of a comparable entity) is compared with the auditor's expectation of what that change (or difference) likely would be. That expectation is developed, in part, based on the auditor's understanding of the entity and the environment in which it operates. Also, the expectation often might be based on information the auditor has obtained regarding matters specifically affecting the financial amounts used in the ratio (for example, changes in prices for major product lines if the ratio uses sales revenue as a variable).

3.43 The expectation developed using ratio analysis often may be more precise than, for example, that developed using trend analysis. In part, that is because ratio analysis is based on known relationships among the accounts or nonfinancial variables used in calculating the ratio. However, the level of precision of the expectation from a ratio analysis might still be relatively low. Therefore, ratio analysis likely would be used to obtain audit evidence to corroborate or contradict evidence obtained from other sources, including other types of substantive procedures. However, in a circumstance in which the risk of material misstatement for the account being audited is assessed as low, ratio analysis might be the principal substantive procedure.

Determining and Responding to a Significant Difference

3.44 Using professional judgment, and taking performance materiality into account, the auditor should decide what level of change in a ratio from a previous period, or what amount of difference from a ratio for a comparable entity, will be considered a significant difference. For example, the auditor may expect that the gross profit percentage for the current year is likely to be 30 percent, compared to 28 percent for the previous year. For this particular audit, the auditor might decide that if the ratio based on recorded amounts is over 30.5 percent or less than 29.5 percent, further audit work would be done to investigate the difference. This decision would be made on the basis that this level of difference may indicate the possible existence of a material misstatement in either sales revenue, cost of sales, or both.

3.45 If the auditor identifies a significant difference, further procedures to investigate the difference might include, for example, a more precise ratio analysis using data at a more disaggregated level to obtain more information on what may be causing the difference. The investigation might also entail, for example, tests of details of various factors affecting the ratio, such as actual sales prices, volumes, and product mix.

Non-Statistical Predictive Modeling

Number and Nature of Variables

3.46 Paragraph .A12 of AU-C section 520 states that, in some cases, even an unsophisticated predictive model may be effective as an analytical procedure. For example, when an entity has a known number of employees at fixed rates of pay throughout the period, it may be possible for the auditor to use this data to estimate the total payroll costs for the period with a high degree of accuracy, thereby providing audit evidence for a significant item in the financial statements and reducing the need to perform tests of details on the payroll.

3.47 In this example, the independent variables (predictors) are the number of employees and their fixed rates of pay. The dependent variable is total payroll costs. To use this model, the auditor multiplies the number of employees by the fixed rate of pay to obtain an expectation of total payroll costs. The model does not involve the use of statistical methods. A statistical method involves using statistics such as averages and standard deviations and, in some cases, more complex statistics involving the use of probability distributions.

3.48 Example 3-1 in appendix B is another example of the use of a non-statistical predictive model.

Developing the Auditor's Expectation

3.49 There may be many opportunities to use unsophisticated but effective predictive models in audits. In the context of the particular audit, the auditor exercises professional judgement to decide the variables to be used and the model to be applied to them.

3.50 Using a non-statistical predictive model generally provides a more precise expectation than, for example, ratio analysis because its use involves the formation of explicit expectations similar to regression analysis. That is, multiple sources of data, both financial and nonfinancial, across time may be used in a non-statistical predictive model.

3.51 Decisions regarding the nature and number of variables to use in the model, and the assumptions regarding how those variables interact, affect the precision of the auditor's expectation. For example, an unexpected difference could be caused by factors not considered in the development of the expectation. Using the payroll example in paragraph 3.46, the model may have used the average number of employees for the year, and the average of fixed rates of pay for some categories of employees. However, to obtain a sufficient expectation, the auditor might need to make the model more precise. For example, it could take into account changes in the number of employees and changes in pay rates that occurred at certain times during the year.

3.52 The expectation developed using a non-statistical predictive model may be, in some cases, highly precise. In those circumstances, the use of the predictive model may be the principal substantive procedure used to address the risk of material misstatement for the account being audited. However, in other cases, the model used may provide a lower level of precision of the expectation. In that case, the predictive model might be used to obtain evidence to corroborate or contradict evidence provided by other procedures performed.

Determining and Responding to a Significant Difference

3.53 The auditor is required to determine the amount of the difference that will be considered to be a significant difference between the auditor's expectation and the recorded amount. As with other substantive analytical procedures, this is a matter of professional judgment for the auditor, taking into account performance materiality.

3.54 If the auditor identifies a significant difference, further procedures to investigate the difference might include, for example, using data and a model that are more precise. The investigation might also entail using substantive tests of details.

Regression Analysis

Number and Nature of Variables

3.55 Paragraph .A4 of AU-C section 520 states that various methods may be used to perform analytical procedures. These methods range from performing simple comparisons to performing complex analyses using advanced statistical techniques.

3.56 Regression analysis is an advanced statistical technique. The regression may be, for example, a time-series regression or a cross-sectional regression. A *time-series regression* uses data from several previous periods (for example, monthly data) to develop a regression model to predict amounts for future periods, (for example, monthly sales data, and data on independent variables ([predictors] affecting sales in previous years could be used to predict monthly sales in the current year). On the other hand, a *cross-sectional regression* uses data for one period of time or at a point in time. For example, in the audit of the financial statements of a retail store chain, a cross-section of relevant data could be used to predict the sales revenue for each store for the current year. Predictors might include, for each store, the square footage of shelf space, the types of products sold, the inventory on hand to sell, the number of staff, the hours of operation, and customer demographic data. This cross-sectional regression would show how the predicted sales for each store differs from that of other stores, based on the regression model derived from all the stores.

3.57 Example 3-2 in appendix B is an example of a time-series regression.

Developing the Auditor's Expectation

3.58 Regression analysis has the same objective as trend analysis, ratio analysis, and non-statistical predictive modelling, which is to identify the potential for material misstatement. The advantage of regression analysis over other methods is as follows:

    a. The regression analysis provides an explicit, mathematically objective, and precise method for forming an expectation.

    b. The regression analysis allows the inclusion of a larger number of relevant predictor (independent) variables.

    c. The regression analysis provides direct and quantitative measures of the precision of the expectation.

Determining and Responding to a Significant Difference

3.59 As with other substantive analytical procedures, professional judgment is used in determining what will be considered a significant difference between the auditor's expectation and the recorded amount. Performance materiality is a consideration in making this judgment.

3.60 Typically, there are three statistical measures of the regression output: R2, t-statistics, and standard error.

3.61 In some cases, one or more of the statistics may indicate large prediction errors (labeled the *residuals* in the regression output). For example, in a time-series regression in which the dependent variable is sales, there may be large differences between predicted sales revenue for a month and the recorded sales for that month. In this circumstance, the auditor might identify and focus on one or more months with the largest residuals. For example, the auditor may choose those months that have residuals greater than the standard error. The total number of months to pick depends on the number of large residuals. The more months with large residuals, the more months that would be selected to achieve the desired level of assurance. However, if there were many such months, this may indicate that the regression is not a good fit for the data being analyzed. The auditor might also consider patterns in the residuals. For example, residuals following the same direction might suggest manipulation of the underlying data.

3.62 The goal of the auditor in performing further procedures on the months identified is to explain why those months are significantly out of line with what was expected. For example, further procedures, including inquiries of management, may reveal that certain events or conditions affected those months. Management's explanations would be corroborated or contradicted by further analysis, inquiry, or performing tests of details.

Documentation

3.63 Paragraphs 1.48–1.56 set out matters for the auditor to consider when documenting ADAs, which may apply, as appropriate, to documenting substantive analytical procedures. In addition, the auditor should meet the requirements set out in paragraph .08 of AU-C section 520. It states that when substantive analytical procedures have been performed, the auditor should include the following in the audit documentation:

    a. The expectation referred to in paragraph .05*c* of AU-C section 520 and the factors considered in its development when that expectation or those factors are not otherwise readily determinable from the audit documentation

    b. Results of the comparison referred to in paragraph .05*d* of AU-C section 520 of the recorded amounts, or ratios developed from recorded amounts, with the expectations.

    c. Any additional auditing procedures performed in accordance with paragraph .07 of AU-C section 520 relating to the investigation of fluctuations or relationships that are inconsistent with other relevant information or that differ from expected values by a significant amount and the results of such additional procedures

Appendix B

Examples of ADAs Used in Performing Substantive Analytical Procedures

Notes:

1. *The examples in this appendix illustrate matters discussed in chapter 3.*

2. *The examples that follow do not address the auditor's approach to considering the reliability of data used in each example. For further information regarding procedures to address reliability of data, refer to paragraphs 1.38–1.44 and appendix D to this guide.*

3. *In the following examples, if a step or procedure noted in exhibit 3-1 in chapter 3 does not present an issue in the context of the particular example, no reference is made to that step or procedure. Also, in some examples, procedures are combined.*

Example 3-1—Non-Statistical Predictive Model[1] for Rental Revenue

Background Information

B.01 The auditor is auditing the financial statements of a small, privately-owned company that owns and manages 10 residential apartment buildings. There are 1,200 units of varying size located in different parts of the same city. Annual rental revenue from these units have averaged about $14 million per year over the past few years.

Step 1: Plan the Substantive Analytical Procedure

Financial Statement Item or Account and Related Assertions

B.02 This substantive analytical procedure was intended to be a source of audit evidence regarding rental revenue. The assertions to be addressed by this procedure were as follows:

- *Occurrence.* All rental revenue transactions that have been recorded have occurred and pertain to the company.
- *Completeness.* All rental revenue transactions and events that should have been recorded have been recorded.
- *Accuracy.* Amounts and other data related to rental revenue transactions and events have been recorded properly.
- *Cutoff.* Rental transactions and events have been recorded in the correct accounting period.

(Note: "Events" refers to, for example, adjustments to rental revenues by means of journal entries.)

---

[1] Some auditors refer to this procedure as a *reasonableness test*.

Assessed Risk of Material Misstatement

B.03 As required by paragraph .26 of AU-C section 240, *Consideration of Fraud in a Financial Statement Audit,* the auditor performed procedures, appropriate in the circumstances encountered in this audit, to respond to the presumption that risks of fraud exist in revenue recognition.

B.04 This substantive analytical procedure was designed to respond to a moderate level of risk of material misstatement of rental revenue. The level of assurance to be provided by this procedure was affected by, for example, the following matters:

- Results of the audit work performed regarding the entity's control environment in light of the presumed risk of fraud. There were no indications of any incentives or propensity for the owners or managers to deliberately misstate rental revenue.

- Results of procedures regarding the design of the company's controls over rental revenue and the implementation of those controls.

- Results of other audit procedures directly or indirectly providing audit evidence regarding rental revenues, including, for example, verification of cash receipts from tenants, confirmation requests sent to tenants regarding rents receivable, and terms of lease agreements.

Nature of the Auditor's Expectation

B.05 The auditor's expectation was an estimate of rental revenue for each month (the dependent or test variable), aggregated to provide an estimate of rental revenue for the year under audit. The independent variables (predictors) used in making this estimate included the following:

- The number of units in each of the company's 10 apartment buildings (internal data from a source outside the financial reporting system)

- The size (square footage) and number of rooms of the units (internal data from a source outside the financial reporting system)

- The expiration dates of leases, in particular, those expiring in the current year (internal data from a source outside the financial reporting system)

- Average monthly rental rates in the marketplace in which the company operates (external data)

- Average monthly vacancy rates in that marketplace (external data)

Desired Precision of the Auditor's Expectation and What Will Be Considered a Significant Difference

B.06 The desired precision for the procedure was performance materiality as determined by the auditor using professional judgment.

B.07 A difference between the auditor's expectation for rental revenue for a month and the recorded amount of rental revenue for a month was considered to be significant if it indicated the existence of a possible misstatement, that when aggregated with other misstatements, could exceed performance materiality.

Type of Analytical Procedure to Be Used

B.08 A non-statistical predictive model was used to develop the auditor's expectation of rental revenue. Desired precision and level of assurance (level of risk of material misstatement to be addressed) were not explicitly incorporated into the model.

B.09 An expectation of the monthly amount of revenue from each of the company's apartment buildings was developed. Units of similar size and number of rooms were grouped. The number of units in each group was multiplied by the average monthly marketplace rental rate for that type of unit. The calculation was adjusted by factors reflecting average monthly vacancy rates in the marketplace, and the expiry dates of leases. The calculations were aggregated to show total expected rental revenue by month and total annual revenue for each of the 10 buildings.

B.10 The auditor used a widely available electronic spreadsheet program to apply the model.

Graphics or Tables

B.11 The following graphics were used:

- One comparing total expected revenue with total actual rental revenue by month (exhibit B-1). The purpose of this graphic is to help identify particular months, if any, for which a more in-depth analysis may be warranted.

- One showing total revenue per building (exhibit B-2). Disaggregating revenue by building provides the auditor with more transparency regarding the possible existence of a material misstatement. For example, it may enable the auditor to detect offsetting misstatements when an overstatement of rental revenue for one building might be offset by an understatement of rental revenue for another building.

Exhibit B-1

Expected Monthly Rental Revenue

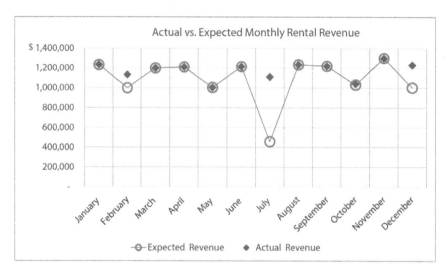

Exhibit B-2

Comparison of Expected Annual Revenue to Recorded Annual Revenue for Each Property Owned

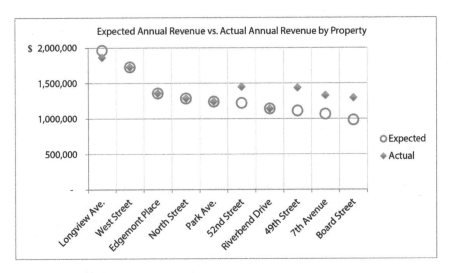

Apply the Substantive Analytical Procedure

B.12   The auditor developed and applied the predictive model for rental revenue as planned. As shown in exhibit B-1, the rental revenues for the months of February, July, and December were found to be higher than expected. Exhibit B-2 shows the particular buildings for which rental revenues exceeded expectations. These differences from expectations were considered significant and, therefore, were investigated.

B.13   The auditor performed further procedures to investigate the significant differences from expectations. These procedures included inquiries of management and obtaining audit evidence to corroborate or contradict responses received from management.

Evaluate and Respond to the Results of the Substantive Analytical Procedure

B.14   The auditor's model took into account that a large number of leases were coming to the end of their term at the end of June. Traditionally, units would remain vacant for at least two weeks. However, in this case, new lessees were found more quickly. In addition, the auditor found by performing additional procedures that significant neighborhood renewal efforts had been made by the city to revitalize areas around the company's buildings for which higher than expected rental revenues were obtained. All new leases were examined to verify that new lessees were, in fact, found more quickly and that the company was able to charge significantly higher rental rates for units in these buildings than anticipated by the auditor's model. Based on obtaining sufficient appropriate evidence, the auditor concluded that there was no material misstatement of rental revenue.

Example 3-2—Regression Analysis of Revenue From Sales of Steam

Background Information

B.15 US SteamCo is a public utility in the northeastern United States. It produces steam and pumps it under high pressure to apartment buildings to provide heat in winter and power for air conditioners in summer. US SteamCo's regulator, the local public service commission, determines pricing, which varies by season and demand, and includes various fees, some fixed, and adjustments for variations in US SteamCo's fuel costs. The schedule is different for November to May (heating season) and for June to October (cooling season). Pricing schedules are revised at least annually.

Set the Objectives for and Plan the Procedure

Financial Statement Item or Account and Related Assertions

B.16 This substantive analytical procedure was intended to be a source of audit evidence regarding revenue earned by the company by providing steam for heating and cooling. The assertions addressed by this procedure were as follows:

- *Occurrence.* All revenue transactions that have been recorded have occurred and pertain to the company.
- *Completeness.* All revenue transactions and events that should have been recorded have been recorded.
- *Accuracy.* Amounts and other data related to revenue transactions and events have been recorded properly.
- *Cutoff.* Transactions and events related to revenue have been recorded in the correct accounting period.

(*Note: "Events" refers to, for example, adjustments to revenues by means of journal entries.*)

Assessed Risk of Material Misstatement

B.17 As required by paragraph .26 of AU-C section 240, the auditor performed procedures appropriate in the circumstances encountered in this audit to respond to the presumption that risks of fraud exist in revenue recognition.

B.18 This analytical procedure was designed to respond to a moderate level of risk of material misstatement of revenue. The level of assurance to be provided by this procedure took into account various matters, such as other audit procedures performed to provide assurance regarding revenues. These procedures included the following:

- Tests of the effective operation of controls over revenues and revenue adjustments (all relevant assertions)
- Confirmation of accounts receivable from customers (occurrence, accuracy, cutoff)
- Various procedures to audit cash receipts regarding amounts billed (occurrence)

Exhibit B-3

US SteamCo: Revenue and Production 2011–2014

		Revenue $	*Production Mlb*	*Cool DD*	*Heat DD*
	Jan-11	23,304,096	659,640	0	1,021
	Feb-11	24,552,000	686,144	0	794
	Mar-11	14,804,728	416,464	0	714
	Apr-11	11,265,320	324,456	1	354
	May-11	5,945,904	151,104	72	114
	Jun-11	10,379,712	479,264	239	4
	Jul-11	13,617,528	708,472	486	0
	Aug-11	14,092,512	687,728	346	0
	Sep-11	12,085,472	567,424	195	19
	Oct-11	11,957,032	392,328	24	223
	Nov-11	10,153,800	254,504	0	383
	Dec-11	15,093,880	358,888	0	662
	Jan-12	22,474,848	566,528	0	846
	Feb-12	18,027,296	473,016	0	680
	Mar-12	14,575,856	410,248	0	438
	Apr-12	9,064,488	264,424	18	294
	May-12	6,582,400	217,264	102	69
Base (Training) Data	Jun-12	10,418,400	499,288	254	11
	Jul-12	14,122,824	732,520	484	0
	Aug-12	14,779,280	725,056	430	0
	Sep-12	12,003,432	608,376	184	9
	Oct-12	4,809,952	369,656	31	173
	Nov-12	7,439,448	192,032	0	591
	Dec-12	18,035,344	420,920	0	681
	Jan-13	20,113,488	531,336	0	899
	Feb-13	23,725,040	587,704	0	851
	Mar-13	20,387,368	505,272	0	755
	Apr-13	17,811,224	427,312	0	366

(continued)

US SteamCo: Revenue and Production 2011–2014—*continued*

		Revenue $	Production Mlb	Cool DD	Heat DD
	May-13	6,082,328	155,032	87	128
	Jun-13	12,064,192	394,400	278	4
	Jul-13	16,033,016	749,152	505	0
	Aug-13	14,311,800	642,688	340	0
	Sep-13	12,291,192	594,184	129	31
	Oct-13	9,845,128	372,080	49	172
	Nov-13	8,933,832	292,648	0	577
	Dec-13	17,613,912	562,320	0	826
	Jan-14	19,228,840	606,400	0	1,123
	Feb-14	26,792,280	714,128	0	938
	Mar-14	19,935,840	805,600	0	866
	Apr-14	13,468,000	375,856	0	412
	May-14	7,344,128	279,296	49	88
Projection Data	Jun-14	11,196,216	517,600	230	0
	Jul-14	13,929,472	749,472	380	0
	Aug-14	12,352,176	663,432	322	0
	Sep-14	12,628,944	701,656	178	14
	Oct-14	9,361,000	411,728	24	166
	Nov-14	10,164,048	293,536	0	579
	Dec-14	18,377,456	567,048	0	752

Nature of the Auditor's Expectation

B.19 The auditor's expectation was an estimate of revenue from sales of steam for each month (the dependent or test variable). The independent variable (predictor) was the quantity of steam produced in 2011–2014. Steam production is measured by mass in units of thousands of pounds (Mlb). This was internal data from a source outside the company's financial reporting system. In addition, cooling and heating degree days (DD) data (external data) was used in the preliminary analysis. Degree days measure how many days outside air temperatures were higher or lower than a specified base temperature over a period. Exhibit B-3 shows details regarding these variables.

Desired Precision of the Auditor's Expectation and What Will Be Considered a Significant Difference

B.20 The desired precision for this substantive analytical procedure was performance materiality.

Type of Regression Analysis to Be Used

B.21   A time-series regression analysis was used to develop monthly expectations of revenue from steam sales. The regression model used is described in paragraphs B.29–B.34. The auditor used a regression tool available in widely used software to perform the regression.

B.22   The regression was intended to provide a level of assurance by establishing, in this case, whether steam production was an accurate predictor of revenue.

B.23   In evaluating the level of assurance that a regression analysis may provide, one consideration is how the standard error obtained from the regression compares to the auditor's performance materiality. In this example, if the standard error level obtained is less than performance materiality, this provides further confidence regarding use of the regression. On the other hand, if the standard error is a high percentage of performance materiality, the auditor would consider limiting how much assurance the auditor intends to derive from the regression. Regression analyses that factor in performance materiality, and the auditor's desired level of assurance, would ordinarily adjust achieved assurance for the standard error.

B.24   Residuals in a regression analysis represent the variability in the test variable (in this example, revenue) that is not explained by the regression model. The statistical results of the regression analysis are combined with the results of other procedures using the professional judgment of the auditor. Other procedures might include further statistical analysis of the residuals.

Graphics and Tables

B.25   The auditor decided to use the graphics shown in exhibits B-4–B-12 to show key aspects of developing and applying the regression model.

Exhibit B-4

Scatter Plot of Revenue vs. Production, 2011–2014, With Regression Line

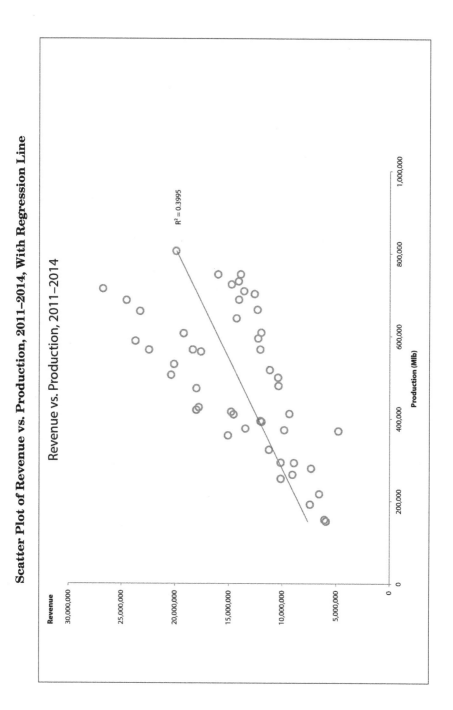

Revenue vs. Production, 2011–2014

$R^2 = 0.3995$

Apply the Regression Analysis

Exploratory Analysis—Understanding the Data

B.26 To start exploring the data, the auditor regressed revenue against production for the entire dataset, 2011–2014, as depicted in exhibit B-4. In this example, the correlation between the variables, measured by R^2 was rather weak relative to the auditor's expectations.[2] The line appears to be averaging between two separate data series. The auditor found that this is precisely what was happening because the relationship between revenue and production differed in heating and cooling months.

---

[2] R^2 is a number between 0 and 1 and measures the degree to which changes in the dependent variable can be estimated by changes in the independent variables. A more precise regression is one that has a relatively high R^2 (close to 1). Determining an acceptable R^2 is a matter of professional judgment. Most regression analysis involving financial data have R^2 values above .5 and many have values in the .8 to .9 range.

Exhibit B-5

Time Series Comparing Steam Production With Cooling and Heating Degree Days

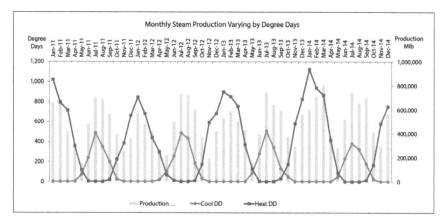

Exhibit B-6

Time Series Comparing Steam Revenue With Production

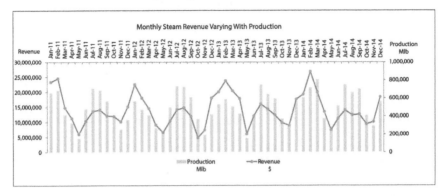

B.27 To better understand this seasonal behavior, the auditor created two time series charts to compare production with degree days and to compare revenue with production as depicted in exhibits B-5 and B-6, respectively. These exploratory charts accorded visually with the auditor's expectations based on an understanding of the entity's business. Production ramps up in winter and summer and winds down in spring and fall. Also, revenues in winter are lower than in summer even though production is roughly comparable.

B.28 With a clarified understanding of the business and data, the auditor began to build a predictive model for projecting revenue.

Exhibit B-7

**Separate Regressions for Cooling and Heating,
Base Data (2011–2013) Only**

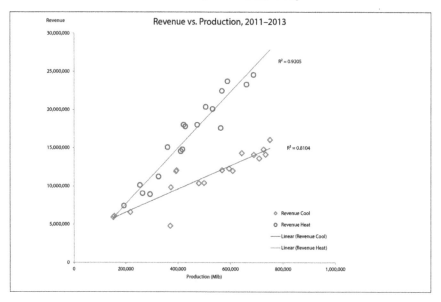

Model-Building

B.29 The auditor dealt with differences in the cooling and heating seasons by treating the observations as two separate data series. To use the analysis as audit evidence (and to avoid circular reasoning), the auditor built the model only from the data from the 2011–2013 base years (that is, not the data for the year currently under audit). Exhibit B-7 shows that the separate regressions provide a much better fit to their respective series than the single regression in exhibit B-4. However, a quick review of the chart reveals an aberration—one cooling month data point is located significantly below the others. Further investigation reveals that this data point is for October 2012, the month when Superstorm Sandy hit the east coast. U.S. steam production was seriously disrupted in that month, and results are highly atypical.

Exhibit B-8

Regressions After Eliminating the Superstorm Sandy Effect
(October 2012)

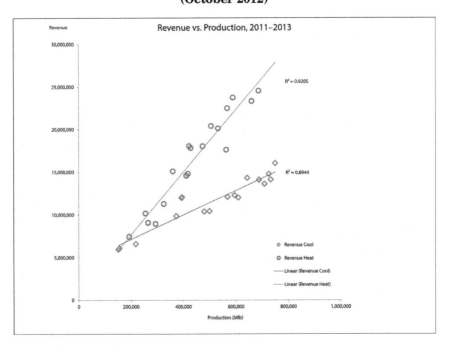

Improving the Model

B.30 The auditor eliminated the anomalous verifiable October 2012 data point to improve the model. The result is shown in exhibit B-8, where it is apparent that the fit has improved for the cooling series, compared with exhibit B-7.

B.31 Additional refinements to the two series might be to add variables that reflect officially scheduled prices. For example, marginal pricing could be used to create a synthetic predicting variable consisting of production times marginal price. Also, other predicting variables could be introduced to account for pricing components that are semi-fixed and do not depend on consumption. A refinement that might be desirable in this case would be to create a dummy variable to distinguish between heating months and cooling months. Such a variable would have the value 1 in heating months and 0 in cooling months (or vice versa). The effect can be visualized as creating a third axis in exhibit B-8. The heating points would be pushed a distance of 1 into the 3-D diagram, and a flat plane would be fitted that runs through the center of both the heating points and the cooling points. In that way, one regression model with two predicting variables would be created, rather than two functions with one predicting variable each.

B.32 Multivariate models in which the test variable is regressed simultaneously against several predicting variables can be an effective way to account for the many factors that affect the test variable. However, this makes the model much more complex. The goal is to include as many variables as are needed, but no more than that, to create a predictive model that credibly explains the behavior of the test variable. A powerful model that is also sparse (that is, having a low number of variables) is the ideal. Deciding which variables and how many is more art than science. Some regression packages (in software) can select such a set, at least according to quantitative criteria.

B.33 For simplicity, this example assumes that the auditor deems the model depicted in exhibit B-8 to be adequate for a substantive analytical procedure. The regression equations based on the 2011–2013 data and depicted as lines in the exhibit are as follows:

- Cooling: Projected Revenue = 14.302 × Mlb Produced + 4,266,060
- Heating: Projected Revenue = 36.699 × Mlb Produced + 345,199

B.34 The auditor used a regression package for these and other calculations. However, the slopes and intercepts of the two regression functions can be computed using functions in widely available software. We can see that the slope of the heating season regression function is greater than that of the cooling season function: 36.699 versus 14.302. This reflects the fact that an additional Mlb in heating season is more expensive than an additional Mlb in cooling season. On the other hand, the intercept term of the cooling season function exceeds that of the heating season function: 4,266,060 versus 345,199. This suggests that there is a larger fixed component to revenues in cooling versus heating months. These coefficients and constants were directionally as expected based on, for example, the results of procedures performed by the auditors to obtain an understanding of the entity's business.

Exhibit B-9

Regression Model From 2011–2013 Base Data With 2014 Data Superimposed

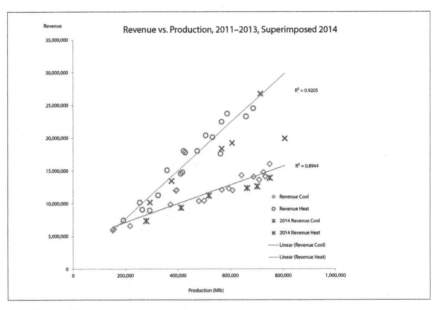

Confirmatory Analysis of Audit Revenues

B.35 Having created the model from the base data, the auditor plugged in the 2014 data as shown in exhibit B-9. For each observation, the difference between recorded and projected revenue is the residual unexplained behavior calculated as follows:

Residual = Recorded Revenue — Projected Revenue.

B.36 Each residual can be represented graphically as the distance (positive or negative) between the data point and the regression line measured on the vertical line rising perpendicularly from the value of the predicting variable on the horizontal axis and running parallel to the vertical axis.

Exhibit B-10

Time Series Plot of Residuals

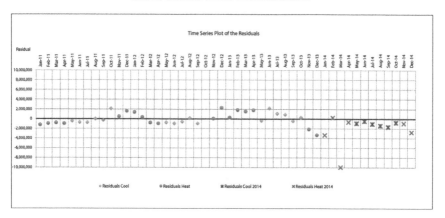

B.37 Residuals represent the variability in the test variable that is not explained by the regression model. Therefore, it is useful to review a timeline plot of the residuals to see if any patterns emerge that might indicate specific missing model elements and also to detect such things as large residuals at quarter or year-end that reverse in the following period. The residuals for the base data used to develop the regression model always sum to zero (because the regression function passes through the mean). However, the residuals for the projection data usually do not. The monthly residuals for US SteamCo are shown in exhibit B-10.

Exhibit B-11

Testing for Significant Fluctuations From the Regression Line

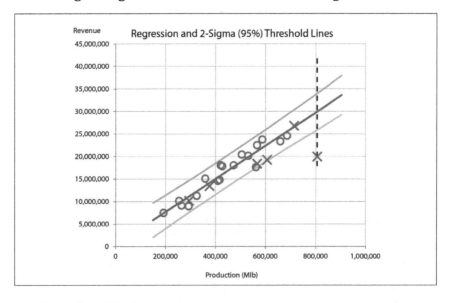

Analysis of Residuals

B.38 The auditor performed an analysis of residuals. Clearly, heating revenue for March 2014 was significantly less than projected by the predictive model. The auditor also determined whether there were other significant residuals by using the statistical characteristics of the model developed from the base data, in particular, the historical degree of fluctuation from the model. It is reasonable to consider a fluctuation as essentially random for any given monthly production statistic. Also, its probability follows an approximate bell curve centered on the regression projection. Therefore, two-sigma (two-standard deviation) thresholds can be established around regression estimates, within which actual revenue is expected to fall approximately 95 percent of the time. Exhibit B-11 shows the regression function for heat revenues, together with upper and lower two-sigma thresholds. Note that the threshold lines in exhibit B-11 bend away from the regression line (two-sigma becomes larger) as the predicting variable moves away from the center of the base observations. In this case, average production in the base period is 441,000 Mlb. At that midpoint, the two-sigma band is at its narrowest as measured on a vertical line perpendicular to the horizontal and parallel to the vertical axis. For values further from the center, projections become more variable and the two-sigma band becomes wider.

B.39 In round numbers, about 800,000 Mlb of steam was produced in March 2014 and the regression model projected revenues of just less than $30 million. Recorded sales were about $20 million, approximately $10 million less than projected. Recorded revenues would be expected to fall somewhere on the dotted vertical line illustrated in exhibit B-11, and 95 percent of the time they are expected to fall within the two-sigma thresholds.

Exhibit B-12

Probability Distribution of Potential Revenues for March 2014

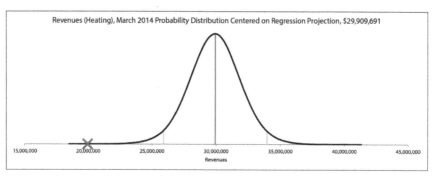

B.40 Exhibit B-12 shows the probability distribution of sales at the 800,000 Mlb point. The distribution is centered on the regression projection, which is slightly less than $30,000,000. Two-sigma at this point on the regression line is about $4 million. Accordingly, the lower and upper thresholds are at about $26 million and $34 million, respectively. Probability is represented by the relative area under the curve. Thus, by definition of two-sigma, the area between the thresholds is 95 percent. The probability that random effects will cause revenues to fall below the lower threshold is $2^{1}/_{2}$ percent. At that level, the fluctuation is statistically significant enough to warrant further investigation. The probability that actual revenue would randomly be as low as $20 million (X marks the spot) is vanishingly small, and it is almost certain that something specific caused the fluctuation.

B.41 The probability distribution in exhibit B-11 can be imagined as sitting vertically on exhibit B-12 with its peak facing skywards, its horizontal axis on the dotted line and centered on the regression line. The distribution is based on a t-distribution with degrees of freedom equal to the number of base observations for heating months after eliminating October 2012 (Sandy) minus two, that is, 16 degrees of freedom.

B.42 The auditor also looked for patterns in the data that might suggest the potential for misstatement, for example, runs of data points above or below the regression line. From exhibit B-12 it appeared that 2014 revenue was consistently less than projected. The auditor investigated this matter and the individually significant fluctuations identified. Procedures performed included, for example, making inquiries of management and obtaining corroborating audit evidence through examination of documentation relating to production and invoicing.

Evaluate and Respond to the Results of the Procedure

B.43 The auditor's expectation was an estimate of revenue from sales of steam for each month (the dependent or test variable). The recorded revenue from steam sales was significantly different from the auditor's expectation. The results of this regression analysis caused the auditor to reassess aspects of the effective operation of some of the entity's controls relevant to revenue and re-design the nature and extent of tests of details to respond to the changes in the assessed risk of material misstatement.

Chapter 4

Using ADAs in Performing Tests of Details

Matters Covered in This Chapter

4.01 This chapter discusses matters related to the use of ADAs in performing tests of details.

4.02 The matters discussed in this chapter are based on concepts introduced in chapter 1, "Introduction." Paragraph 1.17 emphasizes the need for the auditor to exercise professional judgment and professional skepticism in planning, performing, and evaluating the results of ADAs.

4.03 The following examples are provided in appendix C:

- Example 4-1—Cash Receipt to Sales Invoice Matching Procedure
- Example 4-2—Three-Way Match of Sales Invoices, Shipping Documents, and a Master Price List

Certain GAAS Relevant to the Use of ADAs in Performing Tests of Details

Nature and Extent of Substantive Procedures

4.04 ADAs are techniques that can be used to perform one or more procedures on all the items in a population. Paragraph .A67 of AU-C section 330, *Performing Audit Procedures in Response to Assessed Risks and Evaluating the Audit Evidence Obtained*, states that the auditor may decide that it will be most appropriate to examine the entire population of items that make up a class of transactions or account balance (or a stratum within that population), when the repetitive nature of a calculation or other process performed automatically by an information system makes a 100 percent examination cost effective.

Implications for Internal Control Related to Identified Misstatements

4.05 An ADA that has been used in performing a test of details may result in the auditor identifying a misstatement. This misstatement may indicate either the absence of a relevant control or a deviation from a control on which the auditor may have intended to rely. Such a misstatement would generally be considered a deficiency in internal control, the severity of which would require the auditor's assessment. Paragraph .16 of AU-C section 330 states that when evaluating the operating effectiveness of relevant controls, the auditor should evaluate whether misstatements that have been detected by substantive procedures indicate that controls are not operating effectively. The absence of misstatements detected by substantive procedures, however, does not provide audit evidence that controls related to the relevant assertion being tested are effective.

4.06 Further, as stated in paragraph .A4 of AU-C section 450, *Evaluation of Misstatements Identified During the Audit*, a misstatement may not be an isolated occurrence. Evidence that other misstatements may exist include, for example, when the auditor identifies that a misstatement arose from a breakdown in internal control or from inappropriate assumptions or valuation methods that have been widely applied by the entity. Also, in accordance with paragraph .A11 of AU-C section 265, *Communicating Internal Control Related Matters Identified in an Audit*, if the auditor identifies a material misstatement of the financial statements under audit in circumstances that indicate that the misstatement would not have been detected by the entity's internal control, then this is an indicator of a material weakness.

Evaluation of Misstatements

4.07 An ADA used in performing a test of details may provide information to the auditor that would be useful in evaluating misstatements detected by that test. Paragraph .11*a* of AU-C section 450 states that the auditor should determine whether uncorrected misstatements are material, individually or in the aggregate. In making this determination, the auditor should consider the size and nature of the misstatements, both in relation to particular classes of transactions, account balances, or disclosures and the financial statements as a whole, and the particular circumstances of their occurrence.

Applying Five Basic Steps for an ADA

4.08 Exhibit 4-1 sets out five basic steps and related procedures for use in planning, performing, and evaluating the results of an ADA used in performing a test of details. An auditor might decide to perform steps and procedures other than those set out in exhibit 4-1 or perform them together or perhaps in a different order.

4.09 Exhibit 4-1 largely duplicates exhibit 2-1 and is provided here for ease of reference. The only differences between this exhibit and exhibit 2-1 are the references that have been made to exhibit 4-2 and the documentation requirements in AU-C section 330.

4.10 The discussion in paragraphs 4.11–4.19 and the examples provided in this chapter highlight for consideration certain aspects of the steps and procedures set out in exhibit 4-1.

Exhibit 4-1

Five Basic Steps and Related Procedures an Auditor Might Use When Using an ADA in Performing a Test of Details

1. **Plan the ADA.**
   a. Determine the financial statement item(s) account(s) or disclosures, and related assertions for which the ADA will be applied.
   b. Determine the overall purpose of the ADA (risk assessment, test of controls, substantive analytical procedure, test of details, helping to form an overall conclusion).
   c. Determine the specific objectives of the ADA (within the context of its overall purpose).
   d. Determine the data population to be analyzed or tested using the ADA, including, for planning purposes, preliminary consideration of matters likely to affect the relevance, availability, and reliability of that data.
   e. Select the ADA that is likely best suited for the intended purpose and objectives.
   f. Select the techniques, tools, graphics, and tables to be used.

2. **Access and prepare the data for purposes of the ADA.**

3. **Consider the relevance and reliability of the data used.**

4. **Perform the ADA.**
   a. If the initial results of the ADA indicate that aspects of its design or performance need to be revised, make appropriate revisions and reperform the ADA.
   b. If the auditor concludes that the ADA has been properly designed and performed, and the ADA has identified items that warrant further auditor consideration, plan and perform additional procedures on those items, consistent with achieving the purpose and specific objectives of the ADA. (Note: See the flowchart in exhibit 4-2 and supporting material for addressing circumstances when a large number of such items has been identified.)

5. **Evaluate the results and conclude on whether the purpose and specific objectives of performing the ADA have been achieved.**
   If the objectives have not been achieved, plan and perform different procedures to achieve those objectives.

Documentation: The auditor should comply with the relevant documentation requirements in generally accepted auditing standards (GAAS) when performing each step and related procedure. Paragraphs .30–.33 of AU-C section 330 set out requirements regarding the documentation of tests of details.

DATA 4.10

Exhibit 4-2

Process to Address Possible Misstatements Identified When Using an ADA in Performing a Test of Details

Using the ADA in performing a test of details
*(Step 4 in the 5-step ADA process
[outlined in exhibit 4-1])*

Evaluate whether the ADA has been appropriately planned and performed and, if not, refine and reperform it.

When appropriate, use groupings and filtering to help identify the following:

- Items having characteristics in common
- Items that are false positives
- Items that are possible misstatements
- Items that are clearly inconsequential
- Items that are possible misstatements that are not clearly inconsequential

Perform further analysis and additional procedures to determine whether possible misstatements that are not clearly inconsequential are actual misstatements.

Information used in the disposition of items to determine whether uncorrected misstatements are material, individually or in the aggregate, considering the size and nature of the misstatements, in relation to the following:

- Particular classes of transactions, account balances, or disclosures
- The financial statements as a whole
- The particular circumstances of their occurrence

Obtain evidence regarding the characteristics of misstatements identified (that is, their nature and effects on the accounts) as well as an understanding of the particular circumstances surrounding their occurrence.

Perform the ADA

Identification of Possible Misstatements and Actual Misstatements

4.11 Exhibit 4-2 provides an overview of a process that the auditor might follow when an ADA used in performing a test of details identifies possible misstatements. Starting at the top of the exhibit, the auditor would initially perform the ADA. Moving to the second box, the auditor would evaluate whether the ADA has been appropriately planned and performed and, if not, refine and reperform it. For example, based on an initial review of the results, the auditor may determine that the understanding of the business process was not complete and needs to be updated; therefore, the logic or model applied needs to be updated and rerun. This is an iterative process, that is, the process of refining and reperforming continues until the auditor decides that no further improvements are needed to the ADA to achieve the objectives of the procedure, or that a different procedure is needed to achieve those objectives.

4.12 The second box in exhibit 4-2 also indicates that the auditor may decide to use groupings and filtering when a large number of possible misstatements is identified. This process is discussed in paragraphs 4.15–4.18. The auditor refines and reperforms the grouping and filtering process until the auditor decides that no further improvements are needed to the ADA to achieve the objectives of the procedure, or that a different procedure is needed to achieve those objectives.

4.13 As noted in the bottom box of exhibit 4-2, the ADA would provide information that the auditor would use to evaluate whether misstatements identified are material, as required by paragraph .11*a* of AU-C section 450.

4.14 An appropriately planned and performed ADA may identify a small number of possible misstatements. The auditor may be able to readily determine that some or all of these items are clearly inconsequential, whether taken individually or in the aggregate and whether judged by any criteria of size, nature, or circumstances. When possible misstatements are not clearly inconsequential, the auditor may be able to manually (that is, without further use of a computerized analysis) perform additional procedures to obtain more information on the size, nature, and circumstances of occurrence of these items. This information would enable the auditor to identify which of the possible misstatements are, in fact, misstatements, and subsequently evaluate those misstatements as required by GAAS.

4.15 An ADA used in performing a test of details may identify a large number of possible misstatements. As noted in exhibit 4-2, the auditor would first evaluate whether the ADA has been appropriately planned and performed and, if not, refine and reperform it. The auditor might also decide to apply a grouping and filtering process to address the large number of possible misstatements identified. A grouping and filtering process could be used as follows:

- *a.* Identify characteristics common to groups of possible misstatements, focusing on their size, nature, and circumstances of occurrence.

- *b.* For each group identified in step *a* of this list, sort the possible misstatements into groups having characteristics in common.

    c. For each group identified in step *b*, perform further analysis and other procedures considered appropriate to determine which group or groups

        i. do not contain misstatements (that is, false positives);

        ii. contain possible misstatements that are clearly inconsequential (in the aggregate); or

        iii. contain possible misstatements that are not clearly inconsequential (in the aggregate).

    d. For the group identified in category *c*iii, perform further analysis and additional procedures to determine whether these possible misstatements are actual misstatements.

    e. Perform further analysis and procedures, as necessary, to enable an appropriate aggregation and evaluation of the identified misstatements.

4.16 Determining the procedures to perform under step *c* is a matter of professional judgment for the auditor. Taking into account the particular circumstances encountered, the procedures performed on items in a group might include, for example, 100 percent testing, tests of specific items, or sampling. When sampling is used, the auditor would take appropriate measures to determine that sample items selected are representative of the entire population of the group, and the results of testing the sample can be projected to the entire population of the group.

4.17 Also under step *c*, the auditor considers both quantitative and qualitative factors. For example, matters may be quantitatively inconsequential individually and in the aggregate. However, the auditor considers whether qualitative factors such as the risk of fraud, management bias, or indications that controls on which the auditor is relying are not operating effectively.

4.18 As an example of how the process in paragraph 4.15 might be applied, assume that an auditor performed an ADA such as that set out in example 4-1 to match cash receipts to invoices. This would be one of a number of procedures used to provide evidence regarding the accuracy of sales. The initial ADA was properly planned and performed and resulted in identifying a large number of possible misstatements, as indicated by various types of mismatches. Under steps *a* and *b* in paragraph 4.15, the auditor's review of the output from the initial performance of the ADA indicated that many of the possible misstatements were in a group related to cash receipts credited to a suspense account. The auditor made inquiries of management regarding the actions they planned to take to properly record the items in the suspense account. The auditor used a further computerized analysis to sort the items in the account by source of posting and other pertinent attributes. This information was subsequently used in evaluating management's disposition of items in the suspense account. The ADA also identified other groups of potential misstatements that the auditor considered to be inconsequential, even if they were, in fact, misstatements. The auditor considered the qualitative aspects of the nature of the items in each group and concluded that no further investigative work was required regarding the items in these groups.

4.19 Examples 4-1 and 4-2 in appendix C illustrate further approaches an auditor might take to address large numbers of possible misstatements.

Appendix C

Examples of ADAs Used in Performing Tests of Details

Notes:

1. *The examples in this appendix illustrate matters discussed in chapter 4.*

2. *The examples that follow do not address the auditor's approach to considering the reliability of data used in each example. For further information regarding procedures to address reliability of data, refer to paragraphs 1.38–1.44 and appendix D to this guide.*

3. *In the following examples, if a step or a procedure noted in exhibit 4-1 in chapter 4 does not present an issue in the context of the particular example, no reference is made to that step or procedure. Also, in some examples, procedures are combined.*

Example 4-1—Cash Receipt to Sales Invoice Matching Procedure

Background Information

C.01 The financial statements being audited in this example are those of a medium-sized manufacturing company that produces goods for sale to a large number of wholesale companies and retailers. This ADA was a test of details to provide evidence of the occurrence of sales transactions and the accuracy of accounts receivable (recognizing that revenue can be recognized only when performance obligations are met). Total annual sales revenue average about $350 million.

C.02 The company's products are delivered on a free-on-board (FOB) shipping point basis (that is, title to goods purchased passes to the customer when a product leaves the company's shipping dock). The company recognizes revenue at shipping point (when control has been transferred to the customer) in accordance with generally accepted accounting principles. For most contracts, the company has no multiple element arrangements. Contracts with multiple elements were addressed separately.

C.03 The company normally experiences a high percentage of cash receipts that are equal to amounts invoiced. That is, there normally are few customer "short pays," billing disputes, or other matters that would result in customers not paying in full the amounts invoiced. As a result, the auditor expects that cash receipts that matched amounts on related invoices will provide useful audit evidence regarding the occurrence of sales transactions and the accuracy of accounts receivable records.

C.04 The company uses an automated bank feed in which cash receipts data from the company's bank and revenue and trade accounts receivable details are accessible with a reasonable amount of effort by the auditor.

Plan the ADA

Determine the Financial Statement Items or Accounts, and Related Assertions for Which the ADA Will Be Applied

C.05 The assertions primarily being addressed was the occurrence of sales transactions and the accuracy of accounts receivable.

C.06 As required by paragraph .26 of AU-C section 240, *Consideration of Fraud in a Financial Statement Audit*, the auditor performed procedures, appropriate in the circumstances encountered in this audit, to respond to the presumption that risks of fraud exist in revenue recognition. The ADA described in this example was not used for that purpose.

Determine the Specific Objectives of the ADA

C.07 The auditor desired a moderate level of assurance from the substantive test of details to be performed. This was determined based on the results of risk assessment and consideration of other procedures planned to address risks of material misstatement in sales revenue and related accounts. The auditor decided not to rely on the operating effectiveness of controls over the occurrence and accuracy of the sales invoicing process. The auditor did rely on the operating effectiveness of the company's controls over cash receipts.

Determine the Data Population to Be Tested

C.08 Because of the key characteristics of the company's revenue described in paragraphs C.02–C.04, the auditor decided that it would be useful to use an audit procedure focused on the amounts of cash receipts from customers (a source of evidence originating outside the entity) and sales invoice amounts for the year under audit. That is, the amounts of cash received related to sales would provide evidence supporting the occurrence and accuracy of sales revenue.

C.09 The auditor obtained relevant data from various files and tables and fields within those files or tables in the company's database. For example, the database had files for invoices generated, open accounts receivable, and accounts receivable cash applications. The data used included the following:

- The company's unique identifier for each invoice issued
- Customer account identification
- Invoice number
- Invoice date
- Invoice amount
- Discount percentage
- Cash receipt identification number
- Accounts receivable cash application amount
- Date of entry

C.10 This ADA was designed to obtain evidence regarding revenue transactions that occurred in the current year under audit. Therefore, cash receipts in the current year related to accounts receivable at the end of the prior year were not relevant data for this ADA. The auditor identified and excluded such receipts from the population of data to be audited by performing an initial automated procedure to match cash receipts in the current year with sales invoices for the prior year.

C.11 The auditor also considered that if the initial results of a test indicated that further investigative procedures were warranted, the auditor would need to obtain data from other database files or tables. These might include, for example, data from the company's sales order file (such as sales order product code, sales order quantity, or sales order amount) and the shipments made file (such as shipping product ID and shipping quantity).

Select the ADA That Is Likely Best Suited for Its Intended Purpose and Objective

C.12 The auditor decided to use an ADA in a test of details as one of the procedures to obtain sufficient appropriate audit evidence regarding the occurrence and accuracy of sales transactions. The ADA was used to compare 100 percent of the company's sales invoices (revenue transactions) for the year under audit with the entity's cash receipts (excluding amounts associated with prior-year sales) from customers received during that year and the period subsequent to the balance sheet dates through the end of audit fieldwork.

C.13 Other procedures were performed to address other relevant assertions for revenue, including procedures to test revenue recognition.

Access and Prepare the Data for the Purposes of the ADA

C.14 The auditor used the ADA to check the numerical continuity of sales invoice numbers to address missing invoices. This helped to identify in advance items relating to cash received from an unrecorded invoice or duplicate invoices. The audit software was also used to identify and address fields with no data or inappropriately formatted data prior to performing the ADA.

Perform the ADA, Evaluate the Results, and Conclude on Whether the Purpose and Specific Objectives of Performing the ADA Have Been Achieved

Exhibit C-1

Example Table: Revenue and Cash Receipts Detail

Invoice Number	Invoice Date	Customer ID	Invoice Amount	Customer ID	ERP Cash Receipt ID Number	Cash Receipts Date	Cash Receipts Amount	Difference (Short) Over	Cash Not Received
1004556765	1/2/2003	8005265	32,568.32	8005265	XX80052	1/29/03	32,568.32	—	
1004556766	1/2/2003	8003256	8,524.65	8003256	XX80066	2/6/03	8,224.00	(300.65)	
1004556767	1/2/2003	8002255	13,325.68	8002255	XX80061	2/1/03	13,325.68	—	
1004556768	1/2/2003	8002136	21,548.77	8002136	XX80068	2/8/03	21,548.77	—	
1004556769	1/2/2003	8003234	5,465.85	8003234	XX80054	1/29/03	5,124.32	(341.53)	
1004556770	1/2/2003	8006851	3,958.21	8006851	XX80059	1/31/03	3,958.21	—	
1004556771	1/2/2003	8007582	4,875.35	8007582	XX80073	2/11/03	4,875.35	—	
1004556772	1/2/2003	8001245	11,956.84	8001245	XX80063	2/2/03	11,956.84	—	
1004556774	1/2/2003	8004387	10,528.24	8004387	XX80092	2/24/03	10,621.03	92.79	
1004556775	1/2/2003	8004312	7,845.62	8004312	XX80078	2/15/03	7,845.62	—	
1004556776	1/2/2003	8001985	26,385.41	*****	XX80060	1/31/03	26,385.41	—	

1004556776	1/2/2003	8009945	8,574.24		8009945	XX80062	2/2/03	8,574.24	—	
1004556776	1/2/2003	8005123	4,784.21		8005123	XX80065	2/5/03	4,784.21	—	
1004556776	1/2/2003	8001147	18,477.11						N/A	X
1004556776	1/2/2003	8006674	6,543.22		8006674	XX80069	2/8/03	6,543.22	—	
1004556777	12/31/2003	8005124	17,543.54		8005124	XX9531	1/27/04	17543.54	—	
1004556778	12/31/2003	8004312	19,652.38						N/A	X
1004556779	12/31/2003	8003234	9,645.78		8003234	XX9569	1/31/04	9,645.78	—	
1004556780	12/31/2003	8002255	3,568.41		8002255	XX9565	1/30/04	3,568.41	—	
1004556781	12/31/2003	8009845	4,778.11						N/A	X
1004556782	12/31/2003	8003336	10,531.12		8003336	XX9534	1/28/04	10,509.45	(21.67)	
1004556783	12/31/2003	8005265	16,654.97		8005265	XX925	1/26/04	16654.97	—	
1004556784	12/31/2003	8002136	29,534.42		8002136	XX9571	2/1/04	29,534.42	—	
1004556785	12/31/2003	8004387	23,568.29						N/A	X
TOTAL			356,027,853							

***** This represents an unidentified cash receipt not able to be matched with a current year's customer invoice.

C.15   The auditor performed the cash receipts and sales invoice matching ADA. The example table in exhibit C-1 represents a subset of the results of the ADA. The data in the table could be filtered and sorted by the auditor to isolate subgroups of transactions for further analysis. The table was also useful in allowing the auditor to reconcile the population of items being tested to the general ledger.

C.16   The results of the detailed table were summarized in exhibit C-2.

Exhibit C-2

Example Summary Table

Cash Receipts/Sales Invoices Matching Analysis Metrics		
Category	Invoiced Amounts Subjected to the Matching Procedure	%
No difference	$306,896,009	86.2%
Cash < invoice amount	16,021,254	4.5%
Cash > invoice amount	4,272,334	1.2%
No cash receipt	21,005,643	5.9%
Unidentified cash receipt	7,832,613	2.2%
Total cash receipts	**$356,027,853**	**100.0%**

C.17 Many items indicating possible misstatements were identified. The auditor followed the process set out in exhibit C-2.

C.18 In this case, the initial performance of the ADA automatically provided groupings of items indicating possible misstatements (cash < invoice amount; cash > invoice amount; no cash receipt; and unidentified cash receipt). The auditor performed further work on each of these groups to identify subgroups with common characteristics relevant to determining the nature and extent of additional procedures to be performed to determine if items were misstatements and, if so, the effects on accounts and financial statements.

C.19 For the "cash < invoice amount" category, a supplementary grouping and filtering process was performed to determine whether the relevant invoices pertained to a particular group of customers or to invoices related to particular product types. The auditor found that most of the invoices falling into the "cash < invoice amount" category related to a particular product line. These invoices indicated possible misstatements related to sales revenue (for example, understatements of sales returns or possible understatements of allowance for doubtful accounts). The auditor singled out the customers in this subgroup for specific consideration regarding requests for confirmation of accounts receivable, including details of the particular transactions giving rise to the potential misstatements. The auditor also specifically considered this subgroup in auditing the allowance for doubtful accounts.

C.20 For the "cash > invoice amount" category, the auditor determined that the risk of cash receipts being incorrectly recorded as revenue was higher than originally assessed. The auditor used the ADA to analyze the data underlying this category in more detail to determine, for example, whether receipts of cash greater than invoiced amounts related to only one or a few customers and, in particular, that overpayments were not incorrectly credited to revenue accounts. The auditor made inquiries of management regarding the causes and disposition of these overpayments and performed corroborating procedures to determine there was no material overstatement of revenue related to this category.

C.21 For the "no cash receipt" category, the auditor again decided to use a supplementary ADA to identify those invoices that matched those in the open accounts receivable table as at the end of the year. The auditor found that all the items matched. Separate procedures were planned to test open accounts receivable balances at year-end.

C.22 For the unidentified cash receipts category, the auditor found that, based on follow-up inquiries of management and looking more closely at postings, most of these were cash receipts related to a few disposals of property and other fixed assets. The company's system was not designed to properly initially identify the nature of these transactions. Amounts related to these transactions were credited to a suspense account included in liabilities. That account had not yet been identified and audited. The suspense account was audited to determine the appropriate disposition of the items contained in it. Further, the auditor concluded that the remainder of the identified cash receipts were clearly quantitatively immaterial, with no indication of any qualitative aspect that would be material for this company's financial statements. The auditor amended the planned audit procedures to identify disposal of assets to obtain evidence that they were properly accounted for. They were appropriately addressed in auditing fixed assets.

C.23 The auditor concluded that the objectives of this procedure to provide evidence regarding the occurrence and accuracy of revenue transactions had been achieved.

Example 4-2—Three-Way Match of Sales Invoices, Shipping Documents, and a Master Price List

Background Information

C.24 The financial statements being audited in this example are those of a medium-sized furniture manufacturer. There are approximately 60,000 sales transactions per year. The company recognizes revenue when it ships goods to customers on an FOB basis, (when control is transferred to the customer). This ADA was a test of details to provide evidence of the occurrence and accuracy of sales transactions (recognizing that revenue can be recognized only when performance obligations are met).

C.25 The company has two main product categories: residential furniture sold to retailers and commercial furniture sold to companies for their own use. There were 7 product groups within the product classes (for example, couches, chairs, desks, tables), and approximately 80 product types among the product groups. These product types described the specific style of a product class (for example, office chair, rocking chair). There are thousands of product variations based on fabric, color, and material combinations. Each specific style had its own stock keeping unit (SKU) number and for each SKU number, there was a separate price.

C.26 Price discounts are granted to only six premium customers having high purchase order volumes. Every sales representative is authorized to give discretionary discounts to the pre-approved premium customers of up to

15 percent off the price set out in the master price list. Deviations above 15 percent requires additional approval of the vice president of sales.

Plan the ADA

Determine the Financial Statement Items or Accounts and Related Assertions for Which the ADA Will Be Applied

C.27 The assertions being addressed by this ADA are the occurrence and accuracy of revenue.

C.28 Types of misstatements that could have occurred include misstatements of revenue resulting from differences among data used in generating sales invoices. These data included, for example, product type, quantities, prices and discounts, data regarding what the customer ordered, and authorized amounts for prices and discounts.

C.29 This ADA was one of a number of procedures used to obtain evidence regarding the occurrence and accuracy of sales. This included evidence obtained from tests of relevant controls and evidence from other substantive procedures, such as confirmation of accounts receivable with customers (including details of invoices) and audit procedures performed in verifying cash.

C.30 As required by paragraph .26 of AU-C section 240, the auditor performed procedures, appropriate in the circumstances encountered in this audit, to respond to the presumption that risks of fraud exist in revenue recognition. The ADA described in this example was not used for that purpose.

Determine the Data Population to Be Tested

C.31 The auditor decided that this substantive procedure would focus on comparing what customers ordered and at what price with related invoices and shipping documents issued by the company. Customer orders were an external source of evidence. However, data in customer purchase orders were transferred to internal sales order documents in a format appropriate for the company's database.

C.32 The auditor obtained relevant data from various files and tables and fields within those files or tables in the company's database. For example, the database had files for invoices generated, sales, and shipments made. The data used included the following:

- Customer account identification
- Sales order identification
- Sales order product identification
- Sales order quantity
- Sales order unit price
- Shipment identification
- Shipping product identification
- Shipping quantity
- Shipping unit of measure
- Shipping unit price
- Invoice identification
- Invoice product identification

- Invoice amount
- Discount percentage
- Date of entry

C.33 The auditor also determined that other company database files would be accessed, including the files regarding the contract process (linking customer purchase orders to the internally prepared sales orders) and the product pricing master file.

Select the ADA That Is Likely Best Suited for Its Intended Purpose and Objectives

C.34 The auditor decided to use an ADA in performing a test of details. It entailed the performance of two three-way matches. For each sales transaction during the year under audit, the ADA was used to compare the following:

- The quantity sold per the sales invoice, shipping document, and internal sales order to determine whether they all matched
- The price on the sales invoice, the purchase order or similar supporting documentation, and the company's master price list to determine whether they all matched

Access and Prepare the Data for Purposes of the ADA

C.35 The auditor used the ADA to check the numerical continuity of sales orders, invoices, and shipping documents and to address missing numbers. Audit software was also used to identify and address fields with no data or inappropriately formatted data prior to performing the ADA.

Perform the ADA, Evaluate the Results, and Conclude on Whether the Purpose and Specific Objectives of Performing the ADA Have Been Achieved

C.36 The auditor performed the two three-way match ADAs. For the three-way quantity matching ADA, no mismatches were identified. This is shown in exhibit C-3, the graphic the auditor decided to use for this ADA. Quantity is shown on the vertical axis of this graphic. There is a different colored dot for each invoice quantity, purchase order quantity, and shipping quantity. The result of this three-way match procedure is that the quantities are the same for each. Note that this graphic might be useful when the number of invoices is relatively small and the graphic could be quickly scanned. For example, when there is a large number of invoices, the auditor likely would use a graphic that summarized the mismatches by customer.

C.37 The results of the pricing three-way match ADA are shown by the graphic in exhibit C-4. In this graphic, the vertical axis is price per unit. A similar three-dot format is used. This ADA identified many pricing differences, as shown by the misaligned dots. For example, the blue dots (list price per the pricing master file) are positioned considerably above the other dots. The auditor responded to this finding by using a supplementary ADA to determine if the mismatches exhibited a pattern of common attributes that would help identify the circumstances in which they occurred. For example, the auditor determined whether the mismatches occurred on a particular date, during a specific range of dates, or whether the mismatches related to only a few customers. The auditor obtained evidence from the supplementary ADA that mismatches were due to the matching process not taking discounts into account. The auditor re-designed the ADA to incorporate a test to see whether any customer, other than a premium customer, received a discount and whether any premium customer received a discount in excess of 15 percent. The reperformance of the ADA revealed no items of this nature.

C.38 The auditor concluded that the client's invoicing process regarding quantities and pricing was consistent with customer orders, providing evidence of the occurrence and accuracy of sales transactions for the year.

Exhibit C-3

Graphic of Results of Three-Way Match Procedures

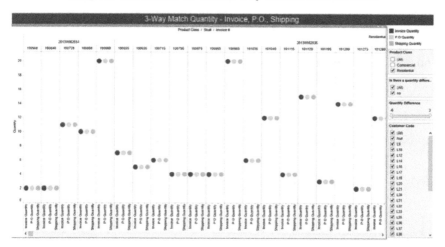

Exhibit C-4

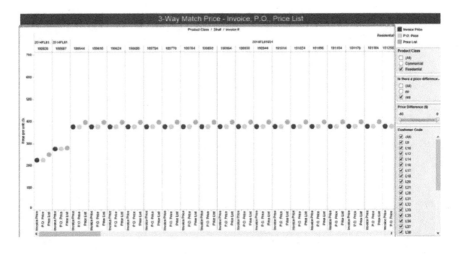

Appendix D

Matters to Consider Regarding the Reliability of Data

D.01 Generally accepted auditing standards (GAAS), such as AU-C section 500, *Audit Evidence*, require the auditor to consider the relevance and reliability of information used as audit evidence. Use of relevant and reliable data is needed to achieve the objectives of the financial statement audit. This appendix addresses data reliability.

D.02 Determining the nature, timing, and extent of audit procedures needed to provide evidence that data is sufficiently reliable is often a key challenge for auditors.

D.03 The matters set out in this appendix are intended to help auditors meet that challenge. These matters include the following:

- Examples of references in GAAS related to applying the concept of data reliability
- Examples of matters to consider in determining the nature, timing, and extent of procedures regarding whether the data used is sufficiently reliable

D.04 For the purposes of this guide, data is considered sufficiently reliable when that data is accurate and complete and sufficiently precise and detailed for the auditor's purposes.

References in GAAS Related to Applying the Concept of Reliability

D.05 Paragraphs D.06–D.16 contain extracts from GAAS related to applying the concept of data reliability. It is important to consider the context within GAAS in which these extracts were written.

Interrelationship of Audit Evidence, Information, and Data

D.06 The terms *information* and *data* tend to be used interchangeably in GAAS. Information is usually considered to be data that has been processed, structured, or presented to be more informative. Paragraph .14 of AU-C section 200, *Overall Objectives of the Independent Auditor and the Conduct of an Audit in Accordance With Generally Accepted Auditing Standards*, defines *audit evidence* as

> information used by the auditor in arriving at the conclusions on which the auditor's opinion is based. Audit evidence includes both information contained in the accounting records underlying the financial statements and other information. Sufficiency of audit evidence is the measure of the quantity of audit evidence. The quantity of the audit evidence needed is affected by the auditor's assessment of the risks of material misstatement and also by the quality of such audit evidence. Appropriateness of audit evidence is the measure of the quality of audit evidence; that is, its relevance and its reliability in providing support for the conclusions on which the auditor's opinion is based.

D.07 Some paragraphs in AU-C section 315, *Understanding the Entity and Its Environment and Assessing the Risks of Material Misstatement*, discuss aspects of the interrelationship of data and information that is ultimately provided in the form of financial statements. This includes a discussion of how the use of IT results in benefits and risks that may affect the reliability of data.

- Paragraph .A61 of AU-C section 315 states that an entity may have complex, highly integrated systems that share data and that are used to support all aspects of the entity's financial reporting, operations, and compliance objectives.

- Paragraph .A62 states that when IT is used to initiate, authorize, record, process, or report transactions or other financial data for inclusion in financial statements, the systems and programs may include controls related to the corresponding assertions for material accounts or may be critical to the effective functioning of manual controls that depend on IT.

- Paragraph .A63 states that generally, IT benefits an entity's internal control by enabling an entity to do the following:

  — Consistently apply predefined business rules and perform complex calculations in processing large volumes of transactions or data

  — Enhance the timeliness, availability, and accuracy of information

  — Facilitate the additional analysis of information

  — Enhance the ability to monitor the performance of the entity's activities and its policies and procedures

  — Reduce the risk that controls will be circumvented

  — Enhance the ability to achieve effective segregation of duties by implementing security controls in applications, databases, and operating systems

- Paragraph .A64 states that IT also poses specific risks to an entity's internal control, including the following, for example:

  — Reliance on systems or programs that are inaccurately processing data, processing inaccurate data, or both.

  — Unauthorized access to data that may result in destruction of data or improper changes to data, including the recording of unauthorized or nonexistent transactions or inaccurate recording of transactions. Particular risks may arise when multiple users access a common database.

  — The possibility of IT personnel gaining access privileges beyond those necessary to perform their assigned duties, thereby breaking down segregation of duties.

  — Unauthorized changes to data in master files.

  — Unauthorized changes to systems or programs.

  — Failure to make necessary changes to systems or programs.

— Inappropriate manual intervention.

— Potential loss of data or inability to access data as required.

Reliability of Information Produced by the Entity Versus Information Obtained From Sources External to the Entity

D.08 The auditor may take different approaches to address matters related to the reliability of data depending, for example, on whether the data is from an external or internal source. This is illustrated in paragraphs .07, .09, and .A32 of AU-C section 500. However, paragraph .A32 warns the auditor that information from external sources may not always be reliable.

- Paragraph .07 states that when designing and performing audit procedures, the auditor should consider the relevance and reliability of the information to be used as audit evidence.

- Paragraph .09 states that when using information produced by the entity, the auditor should evaluate whether the information is sufficiently reliable for the auditor's purposes, including, as necessary, in the following circumstances:

  a. Obtaining audit evidence about the accuracy and completeness of the information

  b. Evaluating whether the information is sufficiently precise and detailed for the auditor's purposes

- Paragraph .A32 states that the reliability of information to be used as audit evidence and, therefore, of the audit evidence itself, is influenced by its source and nature and the circumstances under which it is obtained, including the controls over its preparation and maintenance, when relevant. Therefore, generalizations about the reliability of various kinds of audit evidence are subject to important exceptions. Even when information to be used as audit evidence is obtained from sources external to the entity, circumstances may exist that could affect its reliability. Information obtained from an independent external source may not be reliable, for example, if the source is not knowledgeable or a management specialist lacks objectivity. Though recognizing that exceptions may exist, the following generalizations about the reliability of audit evidence may be useful:

  — The reliability of audit evidence is increased when it is obtained from independent sources outside the entity.

  — The reliability of audit evidence that is generated internally is increased when the related controls, including those over its preparation and maintenance, imposed by the entity, are effective.

  — Audit evidence obtained directly by the auditor (for example, observation of the application of a control) is more reliable than audit evidence obtained indirectly or by inference (for example, inquiry about the application of a control).

— Audit evidence in documentary form, whether paper, electronic, or other medium, is more reliable than evidence obtained orally (for example, a contemporaneously written record of a meeting is more reliable than a subsequent oral representation of the matters discussed).

— Audit evidence provided by original documents is more reliable than audit evidence provided by photocopies, facsimiles, or documents that have been filmed, digitized, or otherwise transformed into electronic form, the reliability of which may depend on the controls over their preparation and maintenance.

D.09 Audit evidence may include information that is not obtained from the audited entity's accounting records or subject to the entity's internal control over financial reporting. Paragraph .A71 of AU-C section 315 states that controls relating to operations and compliance objectives also may be relevant to an audit if they relate to data the auditor evaluates or uses in applying audit procedures. The following two examples may be relevant to an audit:

- Controls pertaining to nonfinancial data that the auditor may use in analytical procedures, such as production statistics

- Controls pertaining to detecting noncompliance with laws and regulations that may have a direct effect on the determination of material amounts and disclosures in the financial statements, such as controls over compliance with income tax laws and regulations used to determine the income tax provision

Performing a Substantive Analytical Procedure

D.10 When performing a substantive analytical procedure, including using an ADA for that purpose, AU-C section 520, *Analytical Procedures*, requires the auditor to evaluate the reliability of data. The requirement to evaluate the reliability of data from which the auditor's expectation of recorded amounts or ratios is developed applies to both internal and external data. Though these paragraphs pertain to performing substantive analytical procedures, the auditor may consider, for example, the matters set out in paragraphs .A17 and .A19 when using ADAs to perform other audit procedures.

- Item *b* in paragraph .05 states that when designing and performing analytical procedures, either alone or in combination with tests of details, as substantive procedures in accordance with AU-C section 330, *Performing Audit Procedures in Response to Assessed Risks and Evaluating the Audit Evidence Obtained*, the auditor should evaluate the reliability of data from which the auditor's expectation of recorded amounts or ratios is developed, taking into account the source, comparability, and nature and relevance of information available and controls over preparation.

- Item *c* in paragraph .A8 states that the expected effectiveness and efficiency of a substantive analytical procedure in addressing risks of material misstatement depends on, among other things, the availability and reliability of the data used to develop the expectation.

- Paragraph .A9 states that the auditor may inquire of management about the availability and reliability of information needed to apply substantive analytical procedures and the results of any such analytical procedures performed by the entity. It may be effective to use analytical data prepared by management, provided that the auditor is satisfied that such data is properly prepared.

- Paragraph .A17 states that the reliability of data is influenced by its source and nature and is dependent on the circumstances under which it is obtained. Accordingly, the following are relevant when determining whether data is reliable for purposes of designing substantive analytical procedures:

  a. The source of the information available. For example, information may be more reliable when it is obtained from independent sources outside the entity.

  b. The comparability of the information available. For example, broad industry data may need to be supplemented to be comparable to that of an entity that produces and sells specialized products.

  c. The nature and relevance of the information available. For example, whether budgets have been established as results to be expected rather than as goals to be achieved.

  d. Controls over the preparation of the information that are designed to ensure its completeness, accuracy, and validity. For example, controls over the preparation, review, and maintenance of budgets.

- Paragraph .A19 states that the auditor may consider testing the operating effectiveness of controls, if any, over the entity's preparation of information used by the auditor in performing substantive analytical procedures in response to assessed risks. When such controls are effective, the auditor may have greater confidence in the reliability of the information and, therefore, in the results of analytical procedures. The operating effectiveness of controls over nonfinancial information may often be tested in conjunction with other tests of controls. For example, in establishing controls over the processing of sales invoices, an entity may include controls over the recording of unit sales. In these circumstances, the auditor may test the operating effectiveness of controls over the recording of unit sales in conjunction with tests of the operating effectiveness of controls over the processing of sales invoices. Alternatively, the auditor may consider whether the information was subjected to audit testing. AU-C section 330 addresses determining the audit procedures to be performed on the information to be used for substantive analytical procedures.

Doubts About the Reliability of Information Used as Audit Evidence

D.11 Paragraph .10 of AU-C section 500 states that if

a. audit evidence obtained from one source is inconsistent with that obtained from another or *b.* the auditor has doubts over the reliability of information to be used as audit evidence the auditor shall determine what modifications or additions to audit procedures are necessary to resolve the matter and shall consider the effect of the matter, if any, on other aspects of the audit.

Types of Audit Procedures Used to Obtain Evidence of the Reliability of Data Used

D.12 The types of audit procedures described in AU-C section 500 (inspection, observation, external confirmation, recalculation, reperformance, analytical procedures, and inquiry), often in combination, may be used to obtain evidence of the reliability of data used. The auditor may also, for example, use the work of specialists, internal auditors, or another external auditor. The types of procedures performed may depend, for example, on whether reliability of data is being addressed as part of a risk assessment procedure, a test of controls, a substantive analytical procedure, or a test of details. The nature, timing, and extent of procedures used is a matter of professional judgment for the auditor, taking into account, for example, matters set out in paragraphs D.13–D.23.

Examples Illustrating Data Reliability Considerations

D.13 The nature, timing, and extent of procedures an auditor decides to perform to consider or evaluate data reliability depend on various factors, examples of which include the following:

- *Readily apparent characteristics of the data.* Initial consideration of the characteristics of the data may enable the auditor to readily dismiss it as unreliable. For example, it may be readily apparent that data used in a marketing campaign for a product is biased. In such a case, though the nature of the data might have been highly relevant to the audit procedure to be performed, the auditor would consider it not to be relevant because of its apparent low level of reliability. On the other hand, specific widely available data, such as amounts of snow and rainfall that have fallen over a period in specified areas provided by the National Weather Service, may be readily accepted as sufficiently reliable for the purposes of the ADA.

- *Purpose and objectives of the ADA.* An ADA might be used in performing a substantive procedure (perhaps a substantive analytical procedure). In that case, the auditor may decide that the evidence to be obtained to evaluate the reliability of data may need to be more persuasive than would be the case if the ADA was being used in performing a risk assessment procedure. However, regardless of the objective of the procedure, it would never be appropriate for an auditor to use data that the auditor knows to be unreliable.

- *Availability of relevant and reliable sources of audit evidence.* In most cases, the auditor is likely to be able to readily access internal data and obtain evidence related to how that data is processed, including, when appropriate, the effective operation of relevant controls. It may be more difficult to access external data and obtain an appropriate understanding of how that data is processed.

- *Extent of other audit procedures performed.* In an instance in which the data being tested is the subject of the only audit procedure being performed over the relevant account or assertion, the extent of the audit work performed to establish the reliability of that data would normally be expected to be greater than in an instance in which the procedure was only one of the procedures being performed on the account or assertion.

D.14 The following sections provide examples of circumstances the auditor may encounter regarding data reliability in planning and performing an ADA, including matters that the auditor may consider in determining the nature, timing, and extent of procedures to perform on the data in those circumstances. Note that for all examples that discuss audit procedures relating to revenue accounts, it is assumed that the auditor has performed audit procedures, in addition to or in combination with the example procedures noted, to assess and appropriately address the presumed risk of fraud in revenue.

ADA Used as a Risk Assessment Procedure

Example 1—General Ledger Account Balance Analysis

D.15 As part of the auditor's risk assessment procedures, the auditor used an ADA to analyze the preliminary balances in the entity's general ledger. The objective of the ADA was to identify significant changes in account balances from the preceding year that warranted specific attention by the auditor. This ADA included, for example, the calculation of ratios using data in the accounts at various levels of aggregation. These ratios included, for example, days sales in receivables, liquidity ratios, and gross profit margins by major product line. The ADA was also used to provide details on the composition of various accounts, including, for example, accounts receivable by type of foreign currency.

Data Reliability Considerations

Nature of the data	General ledger account balances and components of those balances at varying levels of disaggregation, depending, for example, on the ratios being calculated using the ADA.
Source of the data	Internal (the entity's general ledger).
Process used to produce the data	The entity's accounting system, which is subject to internal control over financial reporting (ICFR). The auditor has tested ICFR and concluded that the controls are operating effectively.
Matters the auditor might consider in determining the nature, timing, and extent of procedures to perform regarding whether data is sufficiently reliable	The objective of this procedure in which the ADA is being used is to provide broad preliminary indications of where there may be higher risks of material misstatement.

(continued)

Data Reliability Considerations—*continued*

Procedures regarding data reliability an auditor may consider performing	The auditor verifies that the opening general ledger balances agree with the closing balances as at the end of the previous fiscal period. The auditor also verifies that the closing balances are those recorded by the entity in their financial statements.
	In this example, the auditor would exercise professional judgment in considering what other procedures, if any, might be performed to provide evidence of the reliability of data used in this general ledger account balance analysis. For example, the analysis might involve preliminary discussions with management in updating the auditor's understanding of the entity and the environment in which it is operating. The auditor might consider, for example, making more in-depth inquiries supported by a review of relevant documentation regarding the nature and volume of such transactions to obtain a better indication of whether the relevant data in the preliminary general ledger balances warranted more in-depth risk assessment procedures to better assess the level of risk.

Example 2—Comparison of Quantities Sold and Prices Charged on Each Sales Invoice

D.16 As part of the auditor's risk assessment procedures regarding the accuracy of revenue, the auditor used an ADA that would plot the relationship between the prices (net of discounts) and quantities for each of the company's sales invoices for the year on a graphic. The horizontal axis showed quantities shipped per each invoice and the vertical axis showed the amount billed per each invoice. The objective of the ADA was to identify risks of material misstatement related to underbilling or overbilling customers.

Data Reliability Considerations

Nature of the data	Data appearing on 100 percent of the sales invoices issued by the entity, including customer account ID; invoice number; invoice amount; invoice date; sales order unit price; shipping unit price; customer discount percent; sales order quantity; sales order ID; shipping quantity; shipping document ID; shipping date; shipping product code; shipping product description.
Source of the data	Internal (the company's database).

Process used to produce the data	The entity's accounting system, which is subject to internal control over financial reporting (ICFR). The auditor has tested ICFR and concluded that the controls are operating effectively.
Matters the auditor might consider in determining the nature, timing, and extent of procedures to perform regarding whether data is sufficiently reliable	The objective of this ADA is to identify invoices in which prices charged seem unusually high or low (including unusual customer discount rates). Such items may indicate a higher risk of misstatement of sales revenue due to management override of controls.
Procedures regarding data reliability an auditor may consider performing	In performing the ADA, the auditor likely would verify the continuity of sales invoice numbers for the year and the absence of any duplicates to confirm completeness of the invoices issued during the period covered by the ADA and reconcile to the total invoices to the trial balance.

Whether the quantity data and pricing data on the invoices are reliable would be evaluated when related controls are assessed and tested, including those related, for example, to the approval of discounts. Obtaining additional evidence regarding the reliability of the quantity and pricing data might also be accomplished concurrently with the performance of substantive procedures, such as sending accounts receivable confirmation requests to customers and sales cut-off testing. |

Example 3—Process Mining

D.17 As part of the auditor's risk assessment procedures, the auditor used a process-mining ADA to help obtain an understanding of the entity's internal control. This ADA involved the use of data in the entity's transaction log (sometimes called an *audit trail*).

Data Reliability Considerations

Nature of the data	Data from the entity's transaction log (for example, the identity of a person performing a function, the nature of the function, and the time when the function was performed).
Source of the data	Internal, part of the entity's accounting system.
Process used to produce the data	The transaction log was automatically generated by the entity's IT system.

(continued)

Data Reliability Considerations—*continued*

Matters the auditor might consider in determining the nature, timing, and extent of procedures to perform regarding whether data is sufficiently reliable	The auditor's assessment of IT general controls (ITGCs) likely would include an assessment of controls over the transaction-logging process. Tests of these controls would be relevant to a number of accounts and assertions and would not likely be performed solely to provide evidence of the reliability of data used in the process-mining procedure. Additional considerations related to ITGCs: • If, as a result of the testing of the ITGCs, they are found to not be operating effectively, the auditor might consider not performing the process-mining procedure, on the basis that it might not provide complete and accurate information that is useful in helping to understand the entity's internal control. • The process-mining procedure could, itself, provide evidence, for example, that the controls over transaction logging are not appropriately designed.
Procedures regarding data reliability an auditor may consider performing	Tests of IT general controls. Other procedures might include, for example, record count checks and linking the log data to the transaction tables to bring in transaction amounts and general ledger accounts and tie out totals.

ADA Used in Performing a Substantive Analytical Procedure

Example 4—Comparison of Units Sold to Prices Charged—Controls Over Discount Rates Not Effective

D.18   This example is the same as example 2, except rather than using the ADA in performing risk assessment procedures, the auditor used it as a substantive analytical procedure to obtain evidence regarding the accuracy of revenue. The auditor compared the units sold with the prices charged (net of discounts) for the entire population of sales invoices issued during the year. The objective of the ADA was to identify misstatements related to the use of incorrect discount rates, resulting in underbilling or overbilling customers. The auditor took this approach because the results of risk assessment procedures regarding the design and implementation of the controls showed that the auditor could not rely on controls over the application of discount rates. Discount rates have a material effect on the amount of revenue recorded.

Data Reliability Considerations

Nature of the data	Data appearing on sales invoices issued by the entity, including customer account ID; invoice number; invoice amount; invoice date; sales order unit price; shipping unit price; customer discount %; sales order quantity; sales order ID; shipping quantity; shipping document ID; shipping date; shipping product code; shipping product description.
Source of the data	Internal (the company's database).
Process used to produce the data	The entity's accounting system, including its internal control over financial reporting.
Matters the auditor might consider in determining the nature, timing, and extent of procedures to perform regarding whether data is sufficiently reliable	This is a substantive analytical procedure designed to respond to an area where the risk of material misstatement is likely to be other than low. The auditor cannot rely on controls over ensuring the proper discount rates are used. This ADA is intended to help the auditor detect misstatements due to error or fraud in the application of discount rates. If the data is not reliable, the objective of the ADA cannot be achieved. However, other substantive procedures would be performed regarding assertions related to revenue that would provide evidence about whether the data used in this ADA is reliable. These procedures often might be performed separately from this ADA.
Procedures regarding data reliability an auditor may consider performing	Other substantive procedures, as noted previously.

Example 5—Data Obtained From an External Source: A Well-Known Government Body

D.19 The auditor used an ADA as a source of audit evidence regarding the completeness, occurrence, and accuracy of sales revenue. The entity being audited was a utility entity that produces steam and pumps it under high pressure to a large number of apartment houses to provide heat in winter and power for coolers in summer. The utility's revenues were significantly affected by weather, in particular, how hot days are in summer and cold in winter. There are statistics related to energy consumption called "heating degree days" and "cooling degree days." Degree days measure how many days outside air temperatures were higher or lower than a specified base temperature over a period. Use of these statistics was fundamental to the effectiveness of the ADA. The external source of the data is a well-known government body.

DATA APP D

Data Reliability Considerations

Nature of the data	Cooling degree days and heating degree days for the location in which the entity operates.
Source of the data	U.S. National Oceanic and Atmospheric Administration (USNOAA).
Process used to produce the data	By accessing the USNOAA website, the auditor found that the government body develops its indexes from daily temperature observations at nearly 200 major weather stations in the contiguous United States. The "heating year" during which heating degree days are accumulated extends from July 1st to June 30th, and the "cooling year" during which cooling degree data is accumulated extends from January 1st to December 31st. A mean daily temperature (average of the daily maximum and minimum temperatures) of 65°F is the base for both heating and cooling degree day computations. Heating degree days are summations of negative differences between the mean daily temperature and the 65°F base; cooling degree days are summations of positive differences from the same base. For example, cooling degree days for a station with daily mean temperatures during a 7-day period of 67, 65, 70, 74, 78, 65, and 68 are 2, 0, 5, 9, 13, 0, and 3, for a total for the week of 32 cooling degree days. Average temperatures are calculated to develop regional data. The formulas used for calculating the averages are available on the USNOAA website.
Matters the auditor might consider in determining the nature, timing, and extent of procedures to perform regarding whether data is sufficiently reliable	The ADA is being used to develop an expectation of revenue for a substantive analytical procedure that would address the occurrence, completeness, and accuracy of revenue. The degree days statistics are a vital component of the auditor's model used in performing the ADA. The source of the data is generally considered to be a well-known and trusted government agency.

Procedures regarding data reliability an auditor may consider performing	The auditor might reasonably reach the conclusion that no procedures beyond, for example, reference to the relevant web pages of the government body might be required to establish the integrity of the source of the data (for example, the independence and reputation of the organization). In reaching such a conclusion, the auditor would give consideration to the risk assessment associated with the assertion being tested, as well as the extent of the other audit procedures being performed over the account and assertions. If this were the only audit procedure being performed, the auditor would likely have to perform additional work to establish a basis for reliance on the information used in the ADA.
	The auditor might assess whether there is any reason that the degree day base used by the USNOAA of 65°F (a widely accepted norm) would not be appropriate for the purposes of the ADA. For example, the buildings to which the analysis relates might be located in a particular region where information available from the USNOAA website or other reputable source indicates that this norm does not readily apply. On the other hand, if the ADA involves data from a large number of buildings in multiple locations, then it may be more likely that use of the accepted norm of 65°F would be appropriate.
	The auditor might also read the government entity's web pages regarding degree day data for any updates regarding the method used to calculate the degree day data. The government entity's website provides a clear description of the basis on which data is calculated, including the basis of any estimates required for certain locations not close to weather stations. The entity discloses any adjustments to past data and reasons they were needed.
	The auditor would also check to ensure that the data obtained is relevant (that is, it relates to the period under audit and the location in which the entity operates).

Example 6—Data Obtained From an External Source—A Private Organization

D.20 This example is the same as example 5, except the utility provides steam to a small number of buildings, which vary significantly in size, structure, and age. Also, rather than the external source of the statistics being a well-known government body, the source is a private organization.

Data Reliability Considerations

Nature of the data	Cooling degree days and heating degree days for the location in which the entity operates.
Source of the data	A private organization that enables customization of degree day calculations and sells an app to deal with many locations simultaneously.
Process used to produce the data	The auditor accessed the website of a private organization that enables the user to calculate degree days using a base other than 65°F. The private website enables the consideration of variables that, in some circumstances, may need to be taken into account (for example, wind speed, sun position, desired indoor temperature, and quality of building insulation).
Matters the auditor might consider in determining the nature, timing, and extent of procedures to perform regarding whether data is sufficiently reliable	The ADA is being used to develop an expectation of revenue for a substantive analytical procedure that would address the occurrence, completeness, and accuracy of revenue. The degree days statistics are a vital component of the auditor's model used in performing the ADA. The source may not be as reliable as a well-known government body.

Procedures regarding data reliability an auditor may consider performing	The auditor might read the website of the private entity to determine whether that entity obtains its data on temperatures from a reputable source (for example, a government agency or a well-known weather service provider).
	The auditor might also obtain information, perhaps based on a website search, regarding the reputation and independence of the entity providing the degree day data. This would include, for example, whether there appears to be widespread usage of its service.
	The auditor might also obtain information from the website or by inquiry regarding the method used to calculate the degree day data, including methods used to identify and make any needed corrections over time.
	In this case, the auditor might conclude that the process used to produce the data is transparent. That is, the information obtained might enable the auditor to conclude that the source of the data is reputable and independent and the entity has no incentive to provide inaccurate or incomplete data. If that is correct, there should be no need, in this case, for the auditor to attempt to assess whether the controls over the process to produce the data are operating effectively. In other cases, the auditor might consider obtaining a Service Organization Control Report® if such a report is available
	The auditor might also make inquiries of appropriate personnel of the audited entity, corroborated by other procedures such as observation, to determine whether the data used to develop the degree day base for use in the ADA is appropriate.
	This is an example of a substantive analytical procedure. In some cases, using professional judgment, an auditor might consider using a similar approach when this type of external data is used in performing a risk assessment procedure because the procedures might involve, for example, accessing information that is readily available on a data provider's website.

Example 7—Complex Non-Financial Data Obtained From an Internal Source

D.21 The auditor used regression analysis as a substantive analytical procedure to obtain audit evidence regarding the completeness, occurrence, and accuracy of sales revenue. The entity being audited is a utility entity that produces steam and pumps it under high pressure to apartment houses to provide heat in winter and power for air conditioners in summer. Steam production data was an independent variable (predictor) used in the regression analysis.

Data Reliability Considerations

Nature of the data	The entity's steam production by month in millions of pounds.
Source of the data	Internal and generated outside of the company's accounting system.
Process used to produce the data	The production of steam involves complex processes that require engineering expertise and need to be closely controlled from an operational perspective. The production measurement process is dependent on different types of meters that also have different properties. There is overall metering measurement uncertainty that is addressed using underlying principles and related equations. In addition, there are many variables affecting steam production data, including, for example, differential pressure, static pressure, temperature, volume flow rate, and velocity.
Matters the auditor might consider in determining the nature, timing, and extent of procedures to perform regarding whether data is sufficiently reliable	The regression analysis is a substantive analytical procedure being used as a source of audit evidence regarding the occurrence, completeness, and accuracy of revenue. The steam production data is a vital component of the auditor's model used in performing the regression analysis. The extent of testing would likely be greater when testing the data underlying the performance of a substantive analytical procedure than when testing the data underlying analytical procedures used as risk assessment procedures.
Procedures regarding data reliability an auditor may consider performing	The auditor would likely begin with obtaining or confirming his or her understanding of the process by which the steam production data is accumulated. This would include documenting the process flow, inclusive of identifying the relevant controls considering the completeness and accuracy of the data. Once the auditor has obtained or reaffirmed his or her understanding, consideration would be given to performing a walkthrough of the process in order to determine whether or not the process functions as represented by management. Based upon the results of the walkthrough, the auditor would gain an understanding of the process and identify risks and relevant controls. The auditor may then decide to test the operating effectiveness of the relevant controls.
	The types of meters used in the process may be subject to outside inspection by a state or other regulator in order to verify the accuracy as of a point in time. The auditor might inquire about how often the meters are inspected, the date of the last inspection, and the results. If possible, the auditor may also consider independently confirming the results of the inspections with the relevant regulator.

Example 8—Internal Financial Data; Auditor Relies on the Effective Operation of Controls Relevant to the Data

D.22 The auditor used a substantive analytical procedure as a source of audit evidence regarding the occurrence, completeness, and accuracy of rental revenues for the period under audit. The entity being audited owns and operates 20 apartment buildings in different districts in a city. Some are in low-rent districts and others in high-rent districts, so there is a wide range of rental rates. There was a total of 2,500 apartment units of various sizes.

Data Reliability Considerations

Nature of the data	Rental rates, number of units, size of units, and vacancy rates.
Source of the data	The company's rental operations management database.
Process used to produce the data	The company used a well-known residential rental management and accounting software package to capture and process the data and produce reports.
Matters the auditor might consider in determining the nature, timing, and extent of procedures to perform regarding whether data is sufficiently reliable	This substantive analytical procedure is intended to be used as audit evidence regarding the occurrence, completeness, and accuracy of rental revenue.
Procedures regarding data reliability an auditor may consider performing	In the circumstances of this example, and using professional judgment, the auditor might decide to attempt to rely on controls to provide evidence regarding the reliability of data used in the substantive analytical procedure. If that is the case, the auditor would evaluate the design effectiveness of the controls and then test the operating effectiveness of the controls over accounting for rental revenue and receipts. If they are found to be designed and operating effectively, the auditor could then place reliance on them. Controls tested likely would include, for example, application controls related to initiating, authorizing, recording, and processing data that is relevant to this analytical procedure (for example, rates, start dates and end dates from lease agreements, and vacancy start dates and end dates). The auditor would also assess IT general controls (for example, access controls and program change controls) that help ensure the effective operation of application controls relevant to the reliability of data used in this procedure. This assessment might be performed to simultaneously address the reliability of data used for other procedures.
	The auditor may also consider engaging a third-party real estate specialist to independently develop rental rates for the relevant districts.

Example 9—Internal Financial Data; Controls Relevant to the Data Are Ineffective

D.23 The auditor used a substantive analytical procedure as a source of audit evidence regarding the occurrence, accuracy, and completeness of rental revenues for the period under audit. The entity being audited is a small, family-owned business. Three family members operated the business, with no formal policies and procedures or defined segregation of duties. The company owns and operates 10 apartment buildings with a total of 1,000 apartments units of various sizes and rental rates.

Data Reliability Considerations

Nature of the data	Rental rates, number of units, size of units, and vacancy rates.
Source of the data	Owner-manager's Excel spreadsheets.
Process used to produce the data	The owner-managers used Excel to capture, process, and store relevant data.
Matters the auditor might consider in determining the nature, timing, and extent of procedures to perform regarding whether data is sufficiently reliable	The analytical procedure is one of a number of sources of audit evidence regarding the occurrence, accuracy, and completeness of rental revenue. In this example, there are no controls that the auditor could test and perhaps subsequently rely upon. Therefore, tests of details would likely be performed to obtain evidence that the relevant data are sufficiently reliable for the purposes of this substantive analytical procedure.
Procedures regarding data reliability an auditor may consider performing	To test the accuracy of the data, the test of details might include, for example, agreeing rental rates to a sample of leases and obtaining evidence regarding the start and end dates of leases. In order to assess the completeness of the information, such as the number of units, the auditor may consider going back to the original purchase agreement for each property and verify the number of units.

Index of Pronouncements and Other Technical Guidance

A

Title	Paragraphs
AU-C Section	
200, *Overall Objectives of the Independent Auditor and the Conduct of an Audit in Accordance With Generally Accepted Auditing Standards*	1.12, 1.44, Appendix D at D.06
230, *Audit Documentation*	1.48–.51
265, *Communicating Internal Control Related Matters Identified in an Audit*	4.06
300, *Planning an Audit*	2.06
315, *Understanding the Entity and Its Environment and Assessing the Risks of Material Misstatement*	2.05, 2.07, 3.13, Appendix D at D.07, Appendix D at D.09
320, *Materiality in Planning and Performance of an Audit*	3.20
330, *Performing Audit Procedures in Response to Assessed Risks and Evaluation of the Audit Evidence Obtained*	1.38, 2.07, 3.04–.05, 3.19, 4.04–.05
450, *Evaluation of Misstatements Identified During the Audit*	4.06–.07, 4.13
500, *Audit Evidence*	1.40–.41, 1.44, Appendix D at D.01, Appendix D at D.08, Appendix D at D.12
520, *Analytical Procedures*	1.07, 1.38, 1.44, 1.52, 2.27–.28, 3.01, 3.03, 3.05, 3.12, 3.19, 3.23, 3.46, 3.55, 3.63, Appendix D at D.10
540, *Auditing Accounting Estimates, Including Fair Value Accounting Estimates and Related Disclosures*	1.44

Q

Title	Paragraphs
QC Section 10, *A Firm's System of Quality Control*	1.11

Subject Index